Contemporary Researches in Hindu Philosophy & Religion
(ISSN 0971-9628)

1. Idealistic Thought in Indian Philosophy; by Shuchita C. Divatia (ISBN 978-81-246-0021-4)
2. Karma and Reincarnation: The Vedāntic Perspective; by Muni Narayana Prasad (ISBN 978-81-246-0022-1)
3. Stonemill and Bhakti: From the Devotion of Peasant Women to the Philosophy of Swamies; by Guy Poitevin and Hema Rairkar (ISBN 978-81-246-0059-7)
4. Śaivism: Some Glimpses; by G.V. Tagare (ISBN 978-81-246-0076-4)
5. Advaita: A Conceptual Analysis; by A. Ramamurty (ISBN 978-81-246-0067-2)
6. Mind–Body Dualism: A Philosophic Investigation; by Alpana Chakraborty (ISBN 978-81-246-0071-9)
7. Hinduism and Scientific Quest; by T.R.R. Iyengar (ISBN 978-81-246-0077-1)
8. Indra and Other Vedic Deities: A Euhemeristic Study; by Uma Chakravarty (ISBN 978-81-246-0080-1)
9. Brahma-Vāda: Doctrine of Śrī Vallabhācārya; by G.V. Tagare (ISBN 978-81-246-0112-9)
10. The Science of Enlightenment: Enlightenment, Liberation and God: A Scientific Explanation; by Nitin Trasi (ISBN 978-81-246-0130-3)
11. Retrieving Sāṁkhya History: An Ascent from Dawn to Meridian; by Lallanji Gopal (ISBN 978-81-246-0143-3)
12. The Philosophical Foundations of Hinduism; by A. Ramamurty (ISBN 978-81-246-0163-1)
13. The Eternal Hinduism; by Baidyanath Saraswati (ISBN 978-81-246-0249-2)
14. Vedānta and its Philosophical Development; by A. Ramamurty (ISBN 978-81-246-0347-5)
15. Sāṁkhya-Yoga Epistemology; by Mukta Biswas (ISBN 978-81-246-0371-0)
16. A Sourcebook of Classical Hindu Thought; by Arvind Sharma (ISBN 978-81-246-0643-8)
17. A Treatise on Advaita Vedānta; by S. Bhuvaneshwari (ISBN: 978-81-246-0707-7)
18. Advaita Metaphysics: A Contemporary Perspective; by Tapti Maitra (ISBN: 978-81-246-0747-3)
19. The Journey of Advaita: From the Ṛgveda to Sri Aurobindo; Priti Sinha (ISBN 978-81-246-0934-7)
20. Theory of Karma: As Interpreted in Brahmasūtra and Bhagavadgītā; by P. Jagannivas (ISBN 978-81-246-1054-1)
21. Fundamentals of Hindu Philosophy of Faith and Morals; by Girdhari Lal Chaturvedi (ISBN 978-81-246-1171-5)
22. Schools of Vaiṣṇavism; by P. Jagannivas and Dayanidhi Kozhiyalam (ISBN 978-81-246-1169-2)

Preface

THIS is an attempt to understand and study the *Brahma Vāda* doctrine of the revolutionary thinker Vallabhācārya (1478?-1530 AD), the founder of the Śuddhādvaita school of philosophy. As philosophical doctrines evolve out of profound, intricately meta-physical discussions for a pretty long period, it is interesting to trace the evolution of Vallabhācārya's philosophy.

It is well-known how man in the Ṛgvedic period was fascinated and mystified at the grand design of Nature, that he wondered if there could be some designer in high heavens (*parame vyoman* as stated in the *Nāsadīya Sūkta*, *Ṛgveda*, X. 187.7). After speculations and discussions, he came to believe that there must be some Ultimate Reality (which they designated as Brahman) as the Cause (or Maker) of the universe. This belief led to a prolonged dialogue of relation between Brahman, man and the world and various views came to be recorded in the Upaniṣads. The dialogue continued unabated in the post-Upaniṣadic period despite the attempts of the *Brahma Sūtra* to synthesize and systematize the divergent views in Upaniṣads.

The discussions in the post-*Brahma Sūtra* period crystalized in three main thought currents about this relationship:

(i) The Brahman, Man and the World are intrinsically one and the same (*Advaita*).

(ii) The Brahman, Man and the World are essentially different *inter se* (*Dvaita*) and

(iii) a sort of a compromise, it regards *cit* (sentients) and *acit* (non-sentients) are different but any how they form parts of God's (Brahman's) person (*Viśiṣṭādvaita*)

> Great teachers holding different views about this relation appeared before Vallabhācārya. To mention a few prominent ones: Śaṅkara (*Kevalādvaita*), Bhāskara (*Bhedābheda*), Rāmānuja (*Viśiṣṭādvaita*), Madhva (*Dvaita)*, Śrīpati Paṇḍit (*Dvaitādvaita* or *Śakti-Viśiṣṭādvaita*).

Against this background, Vallabhācārya's special contribution to philosophic thought is worth considering. Vallabha is a staunch Vaiṣṇava Advaitin. The Brahman or Kṛṣṇa is one without a second. By His sheer will-power He creates, sustains and withdraws within Himself the world. The world is not destroyed. He does not want any *upādāna* (material or instrument) or māyā for creation etc. of the world. Hence, the term *śuddhādvaita*; '*Advaita* not *soiled* with māyā.' Kṛṣṇa transforms Himself into the sentient and insentient world (fundamentals of *BrahmaVāda)* and as such *the world is real*. This transformation effects no change in Him (*avikṛta pariṇāma vāda*). Kṛṣṇa is impartial in dispensing the fruits of *karmas* to individuals. Vallabha rejects the *adṛṣṭa* theory.

Vallabha was an exponent of a special type of Bhakti called *Puṣṭi Bhakti*. For Puṣṭi Bhaktas Kṛṣṇa is partial (principal of Election) and He gives them a special body in *mokṣa*. None can attain to *mokṣa* without Lord's grace (*anugraha)*.

As will be seen in this book, Vallabha's doctrine about Kṛṣṇa and His powers etc. has a close similarity with many tenets of Kāśmīr Śaivism.

But Vallabha's special doctrine of *Akṣara Brahman* needs deeper consideration as historians of Indian philosophy have simply ignored it.

Vallabhācārya's teaching has special relevance to modern tension-ridden world. Vallabha's theory about the reality of the world as against Śaṅkara's theory of world as an illusion, his emphasis on implicit faith in God and his doctrine of *Bhakti-Karma-Samuccaya* will certainly offer solace and guidance to persons of all sects and communities.

Lastly I sincerely and gratefully thank the eminent Vallabhite scholar (and a descendant of Mahāprabhu Vallabhācārya) Goswami

Shyam Manoharlalji for kindly helping me with necessary references and for scanning every line of this book.

I am very much thankful to Shri Susheel K. Mittal, the Director of D.K. Printworld (P) Ltd. and his staff for producing this beautiful book with such promptness.

06.06.98 **G. V. Tagare**

Contents

Introduction

It was one of the darkest periods in the history of India. The Golden Age — the result of the great contributions of ancient sages, kings and agro-mercantile communities passed into hoary antiquities. The memory of that period led to lethargy, a sort of mental stupor. Indians forgot that the traditional memory about mountains Meru, Nīla, Śveta is not mythology but a reality. Thus, mountain Meru is the Pāmīr mount. Nīla is a chain of Zerafshan, Trans Alai, Tien-shan range and mount Śveta is the mountain range of Nura-Turkistan-Akshai Iraq hills. They had a hazy idea about the locations of the countries like Supārśva (Kirghizia), Uttar Kuru (Western Siberia), Bhadra Varṣa (N. China) and the like.[1] In their self-complacency and total indifference to their rich heritage, they became so short-sighted that in their Purāṇas — especially in the *Tīrtha Yātrā* sections, they claimed that all great mythological events and all *Tīrthas* (sacred places) in the world concentrated in their particular place. One wonders why the last redactor of the *Skanda Purāṇa* did not suspect the veracity of the accounts given in the *Revā Khaṇḍa*, *Nāgara Khaṇḍa* and *Prabhāsa Khaṇḍa* each claiming, Broach, Vaḍnagar and Prabhāsa (Sorati Somanath) as the stage of all the mythological events.

This ostrich-like self-complacency led the Indians of the post-fifth century AD period, to ignore completely the social and religious revolution and military progress in the neighbouring countries in Central and West Asia. The progressive research in material (and positive) sciences recorded by Varāha-Mihira in the *Bṛhat-Saṁhitā* (AD 505) was neglected in the mistaken glorification of and loss of the sense of proportion regarding the so-called spiritual or other-worldly lores. Even the 'left-handed' obnoxious Tāntric practices of Buddhists, Śaivas or Śāktas fascinated the public mind. People believed in the self-professed

Of these saints and philosophers, Vallabhācārya was one of the prominent ones.

Notes

1. For the identification of Purāṇic places, see S.M. Ali: *The Geography of the Purāṇas* (Peoples Publishing House, Bombay 1973) Ch. III.
2. Summarised from *The Delhi Sultanate*, pp. 617-23. In the series *History and Culture of Indian People*, Vol. VI, Bharatiya Vidya Bhavan, Mumbai Vallabhācārya states in *Kṛṣṇāśraya*:

   म्लेच्छाक्रान्तेषु देशेषु पापैकनिलयेषु च ।

   सत्पीडाव्यग्रलोकेषु कृष्ण एव गतिर्मम।।
3. अनिन्द्या योषितः सर्वा नैता दुष्यन्ति कर्हिचित्।

   मासि मासि रजो ह्यासां दुष्कृतानपकर्षनि।

   स्कन्द, नागरखण्ड, 144.130
4. स्त्रियो देवाः स्त्रियः प्राणाः, स्त्रिय एव हि भूषणम् ।

   स्त्रीणां निन्दा न कर्तव्या, न चताः क्रोधयेदपि।।

   शक्तिसङ्गमतन्त्र, ताराखण्ड, 23.10
5. For the nefarious activities of *sūfīs* see,

   (i) Sethu Madhavrao Pagdee — *Sūfī Sampradāya*

   (ii) N.R. Phatak: *Eknath, Vāṅmaya ānī kārya*, pp. 6-10.

1

Vallabhācārya: A Life-Sketch

FOR the proper understanding and appreciation of any great person — be he a poet, an artist or a philosopher — some information about important facts regarding his family background and life helps us to understand the greatness or otherwise of his contribution. They explain why he or she adopted a particular world-view. Hence, the need of the life-sketch of a revolutionary thinker like Vallabhācārya.

Vallabhācārya was a Telugu brāhmaṇa from Andhra Pradesh. The family belonged to the *Taittirīya* Branch of the Black (*Kṛṣṇa*) *Yajurveda*. The *sūtra* of his family was Āpastaṁba and the *gotra* was Bhāradvāja. His native place was Kankarwad in Telaṅganā. It is reported that five generations preceding Vallabhācārya, performed a total number of one hundred Soma-sacrifices. Hence, they came to be called *dīkṣita*. Devotion to Kṛṣṇa (with Kṛṣṇa as the family deity) was as if the family legacy of Vallabhācārya.

The names of Vallabhācārya's parents were Lakṣmaṇa Bhaṭṭa and Illammagaru. Like many other scholars all over India, Lakṣmaṇa Bhaṭṭa was gravitated to Vārāṇasī. Being a Vedic scholar and expert in the ritualistic performance of sacrifices, Lakṣmaṇa Bhaṭṭa soon established himself in Vārāṇasī. But those were very precarious days, especially to the inhabitants of sacred places. Vārāṇasī was the special target of Muslim rulers down to the death of Aurangazeb (AD 1707). Rise and spread of Marāṭhā power completely put an end to such troubles.

It was sometime in AD 1478 (1481?) that there was a strong rumour that a Muslim invasion of Vārāṇasī was imminent. Naturally Lakṣmaṇa Bhaṭṭa fled to the south along with his family and friends. Lakṣmaṇa Bhaṭṭa's wife was advanced in pregnancy. The mental tension caused by compulsorily leaving everything at home and flying for life and the physical strain of actually travelling with utmost speed, told upon Illammagaru's health and she delivered on the way a silent child, while their companions were in a hurry to go away as far as possible. Lakṣmaṇa Bhaṭṭa left the child under a tree and with a heavy heart, the couple proceeded to catch up with their fellow travellers.

But imponderable are the ways of the Almighty. After going for a short distance, the motherly instinct of Illammagaru forced her to have a look at her silent-born child. And lo! the child was pulsating with life. Thus, like Gautama Buddha, was born another philospher under a tree in a forest.

Though there is a difference of opinion about the exact birthdate of Vallabhācārya (*Saṁvat* 1529 or 1535), the majority believe that Vallabhācārya was born on Sunday, the eleventh lunar day of the dark half of Vaiśākha, *Saṁvat* 1535. When peace returned after some days, the family came back to Vārāṇasī. When Vallabhācārya was five-years-old, his *mauñjī bandhana* (Institution of the sacred thread and initiation in to *gāyatrī mantram*) was performed by his father. For his early education, Vallabhācārya was entrusted with Viṣṇucitta.

As stated above, Vārāṇasī was always under the threat of Muslim invasions. Lakṣmaṇa Bhaṭṭa thought it prudent to return to the south to Vijayanagar where his brother-in-law, wife's brother, was an influential government official as *dānādhyakṣa*. Vijayanagar was the only Hindu Kingdom which maintained its independence with dignity, despite the invasions of neighbouring Muslim powers. Lakṣmaṇa Bhaṭṭa hoped that he could live there in safety and with dignity and arrange for the advanced education of his son Vallabhācārya. With these fond hopes, the family started on their journey to Vijayanagar. Unfortunately, as Fate would have it, Lakṣmaṇa Bhaṭṭa passed away on the way. Ultimately Vallabhācārya and his mother reached Vijayanagar and stayed with his maternal uncle.

Vijayanagar was a centre of advanced Hindu laerning. It was a powerful centre of Mādhva Vaiṣṇavism. Madhva, the great dualistic philosopher, belonged to Karnataḳ of which Vijayanagar was the capital. Naturally eminent teachers like Mādhavendra Yati, Tirummalaya, under whom Vallabhācārya studied, were Mādhvas. This explains the influence of Madhva on Vallabhācārya whose works *Aṇu Bhāṣya, Bhāgavatārtha Prakaraṇa* remind one of similar titles of Madhva's works.

We do not know which works Vallabhācārya studied under these eminent teachers. Nor do we know, when he completed his education. But in AD 1488, he left with his mother for a pilgrimage. After visiting his ancestral native place (Kankarwad), he went to Jagannātha Purī (Orissa) to attend a *dharma-sabhā* convened there. It seems that even in his early youth, Vallabhācārya attained sufficient mastery in Śāstric learning which enabled him to participate in conferences of scholars. On account of his mastery over *dharma śāstra* at such a young age, they called him *Bāla Sarasvatī*. It is possible that due to his participation in the *dharma-sabhā*, his convictions about *Kṛṣṇa-bhakti* were confirmed. His articles of faith were very simple:

1. The *summum bonum* (essence) of all *śāstras* is the *Bhagavad Gītā*.
2. The highest divinity is Kṛṣṇa, the son of Devakī.
3. Kṛṣṇa's name(s) is the only sacred most of all the *mantras*.
4. (The only) *karma* (or ritualistic work) is the service of that Lord.

Vallabhācārya tells us that it was Lord Jagannātha Himself who wrote down in His own hand, the above orders in a Sanskrit verse.[1] These firm convictions were repeated by Vallabhācārya in his first work *Tattivārtha-dīpa-nībandha.*[2]

After that *dharma-sabhā*, Vallabhācārya went to Ujjain in AD 1489, as there was the *kuṁbha parvan* on the first day of Caitra at Ujjain. After this visit to Ujjain, he returned to Vijayanagar to resume his studies.

Before adopting the life of a recluse (*saṁnyāsin*), he entrusted his two young sons Gopināthjī and Viṭṭhalanāthjī to the care of his trusted disciple Dāmodardās Harṣāni.

After becoming a *saṁnyāsin*, Vallabhācārya went from Prayāga to Vārāṇasī to Hanumān Ghāṭ. There in the presence of the members of his family, disciples, Vaiṣṇavas and others, Vallabhācārya entered the Gaṅgā and took *jala samādhi* in AD 1530 (*Saṁvat* 1587, 3rd lunar day in the bright half of Āṣāḍha). They say that a supreme heavenly light was seen going up from the Gaṅgā. In *puṣṭi mārga*, they call it *asura vyāmoha līlā*.

In his last message, to put it briefly[3], Vallabhācārya exhorts that Lord Kṛṣṇa is not an ordinary god. We entrust ourselves to Him for our good here and hereafter. Kṛṣṇa, the Lord of Gopīs, should always be served by us.

Lastly, it may be noted that though Vallabhācārya was a staunch devotee of Kṛṣṇa, he knew that Śiva is another name of the *Brahman*. Hence, he invokes Mahādeva (Kāśī Viśveśvara) to be witness to his refutation of the *māyā-vāda* in his work *Patrāvalaṁbana*.[4] Vallabhācārya further expresses his hope in the same work, that god Mahādeva, the Lord of Kāśī, will be pleased by his establishment of the *Brahma-Vāda*.[5]

I have specifically mentioned this to dispel the misunderstanding that Vallabhācārya. was a fanatic Vaiṣṇava. There is no scope for such a narrow-minded outlook in the *Brahma-Vāda* as Kṛṣṇa and Śiva are mere different designations or synonyms of the *Brahman*.

Notes

1. एकं शास्त्रं देवकीपुत्रगीतम्।
   एको देवो देवकीपुत्र एव।।
   मन्त्रोऽप्येकस्तस्य नाभानि यानि।
   कर्माप्येकं तस्य देवस्य सेवा।।

2. The following verse from *Tattvārtha-dīpa-nibandha* (*TDN*) is supposed to refer to the above verse of Lord Jagannātha.

भगवच्छास्त्रमाज्ञाय विचार्य च पुनः पुनः।
यदुक्तं हरिणा पश्चात् सन्देह-विनिवृत्तये।।
— *तत्त्वार्थ-दीप-निबन्ध*, 1.3

3. न लौकिकः प्रभुः कृष्णो मनुते नैव लौकिकम्।
भावस्तत्राप्यस्मदीयः सर्वस्वश्चैहिकश्च सः।।
परलोकश्च तेनायं सर्वभावेन सर्वथा।
सेव्यः स एव गोपीशो विधास्यत्यखिलं हि नः।।

4. श्रीकृष्णास्य प्रसादेन मायावादो निराकृतः।
अवैदिकः, महादेवस्तत्र साक्षी न संशयः।।
— *पत्रावलम्बन*, Verses 34B, 35A

5. स्थापितो ब्रह्मवादो हि सर्व-वेदान्त-गोचरः।
काशीपतिस्त्रिलोकेशो महादेवस्तु तुष्यतु।।
— *पत्रावलम्बन*, Verses 36B, 37A

(3) *Difference (Bheda)*: *Bheda-pratyakṣa*, i.e., difference between God and the soul is a matter of experience. This has been accepted both by Siddhānta Śaivas and Vaiṣṇava Dualists.

The *Brahma Sūtra* (*BrSū*) 4.4.17 states that released souls have all powers (of the Lord) except those of creation, sustenance and destruction of the world.[2]

They argue: If in the *mokṣa* stage, the individuality is retained as distinct from the Lord, it needs no argument to prove that they (individual souls) are distinctly different from God in the stage of bondage.

(4) God alone is *svatantra* (absolutely free), others (individual souls) are dependent on God.

The above comparison showing the identity of views in Śaiva and Vaiṣṇava Dualism is enough to show how dualistic Śaivas and Vaiṣṇavas agree on certain fundamental concepts, though there are some differences in details among them.

It need not be supposed that Śaiva and Vaiṣṇava thinkers of the same — *ism* or thought-pattern agreed *in toto* in all details. Thus Śaiva Monist — the *Īśvarādvaya-vādī* school of Kashmir Śaivism holds that the fundamental principle called Śiva is not only Universal consciousness but also the supreme spiritual power. This Highest Reality, the Absolute, is both transcendental (*viśvottīrṇa*) and immanent (*viśvamaya*). It is both *prakāśa* (Knowledge) as well as *vimarśa* (difficult to translate adequately), though tentatively translated as Power or *śakti*. It can create the Universe by sheer Will-Power without any *upādāna* (material cause). But according to the Vaiṣṇava Monist — of Śrī Śaṅkara's school, the Highest Reality (*Para-Brahman*) is mere *prakāśa* (Knowledge). By itself, it has no power of creation unless it is associated with *avidyā* (Nescience). Abhinavagupta criticises this view as follows:[3]

> If the Highest Reality did not manifest itself in infinite variety but remained cooped up in its solid singleness, it would neither be the Highest Power nor Consciousness but something inert like a jar.
>
> *Tantrāloka,* iii.100

I stated that Śaṅkara was a Vaiṣṇava on the strength of his *guru-paramparā* (line of spiritual teachers) which starts from Viṣṇu, as follows:

> Viṣṇu — Brahmā — Parāśara — Vyāsa — Śuka — Gauḍapāda — Govinda Yati — Śaṅkara.

It is interesting to note that Vallabhācārya expresses a view similar to Kashmir Śaivas. While commenting on *BrSū*, 1.1.2, he says.[4]

> The fact of the *Brahman* being omniscient and omnipotent can be proved only if it is uncontrolled and independent Agent of the world.

Again on *BrSū*, 1.1.3.:

> The Brahman is both the inherent cause (*samavāyi kartṛ*) and the instrumental cause (*nimitta kartṛ*), otherwise it will not have complete independence in the power of Action or Knowledge.[5]

Another point of similarity between Kashmir Śaivas and Vallabha is about the nature of the world. Śaivas say that as Śiva is real, His action, the world, is real. Vallabhācārya commenting on *BrSū*, 2.1.14 says:

> The *Brahman* is *abhinna-nimittopādāna-kāraṇa* (Non-differentiated Instrumental — Material cause). As the cause, viz., the *Brahman* is real, the Effect (the world) too is real as there is no difference between the Cause and the Effect.

BrSū, 2.1.15 states:

> The non-difference of them (cause and effect, results) from words like beginning and others.[6]

The *sūtra* is very important as it is based on the *Chāndogya Upaniṣad*[7] 6.1.4. The purport of the Śruti is to establish one-ness or non-difference between the Cause and the Effect. Vallabhācārya positively notes in the commentary of the above *sūtra*, the non-difference between the effect (*kārya*) and the cause (*kāraṇa*).

I wish to point out that when there is a similarity of the thought in two different schools, it is not necessarily borrowed — Kashmir Śaivas based their philosophy on their twenty-eight-Śaiva Āgamas, while Vallabhācārya recognizes (1) *Upaniṣads*, (2) *Bhagavad Gītā*, (3) *Brahma Sūtra* and (4) *Śrīmad Bhāgavata* as the authorities.

It is an important characteristic of Indian authors, Vedists and non-Vedists, that they do not refer to or mention authors of their brother sects (for example, Śvetāṁbara and Digaṁbara Jains) even by name, much less about borrowing from them. Now I shall take an instance of Rāmānuja, the Vaiṣṇava Viśiṣṭādvaitin and Śrīkaṇṭha, a Śaiva Viśiṣṭādvaitin. A curiouss thing is that the Vaiṣṇava Rāmānuja tried to synthesize Vaiṣṇava Āgamas and Vedic texts while Śrīkaṇṭha whose Śaivism was based on twenty-eight Śaiva Āgamas based his *bhāṣya* on the *BrSū*, purely on Vedic texts. He called it *Brahma-Mīmāṁsā-Bhāṣya*. Both were followers of the same philosophy, it was natural that they should agree with each other in a number of views. But in the Introduction, Śrīkaṇṭha avers that his is the Upaniṣadic Mīmāṁsā. His *bhāṣya* is the essence of all Upaniṣads.[8]

S.S. Sūryanārāyaṇa Śāstri has given a list of *sūtras* showing the concurrence of views of those *bhāṣya-kāras* (see Appendix to his book *Śivādvaita of Śrīkaṇṭha*). But that does not mean that Śrīkaṇṭha does not differ from Rāmānuja in the interpretation of the *BrSū*, For example, in describing the process of death, the *BrSū*, 4.2.1. says that *vāk* (speech, i.e., power of speech) merges into the mind. In interpreting this *sūtra*, Rāmānuja says that *laya* is 'association' and not merger and quotes *Chāndogya Upaniṣad* (6.8.6) in support of it.[9] Śaṅkara interprets *laya* as *vṛtti-laya* (the merging of the power of speech).[10] It is interesting to note that Śrīkaṇṭha follows Śaṅkara and explains that *laya* is not *svarūpa-laya* but *vṛtti-laya*.[11] There are also other differences.[12]

These *ācaryas* regarded the same texts as authorities.

Śruti: The Basis of all-isms

It is interesting to note that all Vaiṣṇava authors (and even Śaiva commentators on the *BrSū*) quote Śruti texts in support of their special doctrine. Thus when the Monist quote

Whatever that is, is definitely the *Brahman*

sarvam khalu idaṁ brahma

— *Chāndogya Upaniṣad* 3.14.1

the Dualist counters by quoting: 'He (i.e. the *Brahman*) is not happy to be alone (*ekākī na ramate* — *Bṛhadāraṇayaka Upaniṣad*, 1. 4. 3) and 'Let me be many. I procreate' (*bahu syām prajāyeya* — *Taittirīya Upaniṣad,* 2.6.1).

All these are genuine quotations. None of these are amended or fabricated (though some *ācāryas* are tempted to 'emend' the Śruti texts to suit their purpose).

The reasons of such contradictory statements are historical. Most of these speculations are the results of discussions held during the leisure period while sacrifices were being performed or in the quiet atmosphere of forests or in the personal heart to heart talks between father and son or the *guru* or *ācārya* and his disciples. Various views came to be expressed in such discussions. Such discussions went on for many generations or centuries and were recorded at first in memory before they came to be written down.

Prasthānas

Prasthāna literally means 'foundation'. Certain ancient texts of unchallenged validity were revered as the foundation of our philosophy. The *prasthānas* are (1) A group of specific ancient Upaniṣadic texts, (2) The *Bhagavad Gītā,* and (3) *The Śārīrāka Sūtra* or *Brahma Sūtra*.

UPANIṢADS

Ancient Upaniṣads like *Īśa*, *Kaṭha*, *Kena*, *Chāndogya* are ancient-most Upaniṣads. They belong to a period prior to 300 BC as only these are quoted in the *Brahma Sūtra* whose date (300 BC) is now generally accepted. May be due to the respect to their antiquity, the speculations in these Upaniṣads, despite their mutual contradictions, were never challenged but were shown to support the theories of their persuasion by clever interpretation by various *ācāryas*.

THE BHAGAVAD GĪTĀ

Attempts were made to bring some order in these various speculations. An attempt was made to systematize them under diferent topics. One such attempt that has come down to us is attributed to Śrī Kṛṣṇa Yādava — a historical person who passed away in 3102 BC — "On the very day, at the very hour, *Kali Yuga* set in", as the consensus of all Purāṇas put it. The existence of the Yudiṣṭhira era is mentioned in ancient texts and even by the Arab Sanskrit scholar, Al Biruni (AD 1037). The *Mahābhārata* tells us that when, at the beginning of the Bhārata War, Arjuna got demoralised on moral grounds, Kṛṣṇa told him some philosophical home truths and encouraged him to fight. It seems that later on, some Vyāsa has recorded those discourses under the headings such as Sāṁkhya, Yoga, *Karma,* etc. The *Bhagavad Gītā* is a fine summary of Upaniṣadic teachings on various topics. The *Bhagavad Gītā* or the 'Song of the Lord' is 'the milk of cows in the form of Upanisads milked by Gopāla Kṛṣṇa for Arjuna'. This best nectarine milk is the essence of Upaniṣadic teaching. *Ācāryas* of different schools of philosophy have written erudite commentaries to show that this text supports their philosophical stance.

By the way, it may be noted that Abhinavagupta, the great Kashmiri philosopher, does not believe in the historical setting of the *Bhagavad Gītā* and regards the Bhārata War as a conflict between Good and Evil. The text of Abhinavagupta is the Kashmiri version of the *Bhagavad Gītā* which is at many places different from the text used by non-Kashmiri teachers. All *ācāryas* regard the *Bhagavad Gītā* as the second *prasthāna.*

THE BRAHMA SŪTRA

This third *prasthāna* is known as the Brahma Sūtra (*BrSū*), as the text begins with the word 'Brahma': *athāto brahma-jijñāsā*. But it is also known as *Uttara-Mīmāṁsā* (the latter half of the *Mīmāṁsā*; the former half is known as *Pūrva-Mīmāṁsā*), *Brahma-Mīmāṁsā, Bādarāyaṇa Sūtra, Śārīraka Sūtra.*

Even after the Upaniṣadic period, philosophical discussions and disputations continued in which thinkers of various schools of thought such as Bārhaspatyas, Sāṁkhyas, Pāñcarātrikas, Pāśupatas, Buddhists and Jains participated actively. There arose a need to reconcile discordant Upaniṣadic views and next, to meet the criticisms of Vedists like Sāṁkhyas and non-Vedists like Buddhists and Jains. This stupendous tough task is credited to have been achieved by one Bādarāyaṇa. The *Brahma Sūtra* became the popular title of the work as the first *sūtra* announces *brahma-jijñāsā*. Later on it became famous as *Vedānta Sūtra*. Its real — original — name seems to be *Śārīraka Sūtra*. H. Nakamura, in *Early Vedanta Philosophy* (p. 426) notes that early authors like Upavarṣa and Bodhāyana record its name as *Śārīraka Sūtra*. Śaṅkara has adopted *Śrīraka Sūtr*a as the name of the text commented upon by him. The word *śārīraka* means 'that which has a body'. It literally means 'the individual soul'. I doubt whether the *Brahma Sūtra* (*BrSū*) uses the word *śārīraka* in the sense of 'the *Brahman*'. I would like to know which *sūtra* in the *BrSū* explicitly states or implies that the body of the *Brahman* is constituted of the *cit* (Conscious) and *acit* (non-conscious and non-intelligent parts). Padmapāda, the direct disciple of Śaṅkara and the earliest commentator on his (*Śārīraka*'s) *Bhāṣya* states explicitly:

> *Śārīraka* is *jīva* and the work pertaining to it is *Śārīraka*.[13]

I do not know what Upavarṣa and Bodhāyana implied by this term.

We are not concerned here with the problem whether *Dharma* (*Pūrva*) *Mīmāṁsā* attributed to Jaimini and *Brahma-Mīmāmsā* attributed to Bādarāyaṇa constituted one *Mīmāṁsā Sūtra*. It is significant that Vallabhācārya wrote commentaries on both the *Mīmāṁsās*.

BrSū was not written 'at one sitting' but it belongs to the category of 'the literature of growth'. It consists of quotations from the *Ṛgveda*, *Śatapatha*, and *Aitareya Brāhmaṇas*. But most of the quotations are from Upaniṣads. The majority of the quotations are from the *Chāndogya* Upaniṣad and next to it from the *Bṛhadāraṇayaka Upaniṣad* (in number). All the quotations are from the oldest stratum of Upaniṣads. Belvalkar in his '*Lectures*' (*Basu Mallik Lectures on Vedanta Philosophy*, Pune 1929, pp. 142-46) tried to reconstruct the 'original' part of the *BrSū* Even if we ignore that attempt as it is a personal opinion of

Belvalkar, the various references in the text of *BrSū* show its period of composition to be *circa* 300 BC as we find that the Upaniṣads quoted belong to the older strata. No new Upaniṣads are quoted.

As the *BrSū* belongs to the category of 'Literature of Growth' differences of opinions, views of teachers belonging to different centuries came to be recorded in the same book. The contents of the *BrSū* are given in the next chapter. The names of pre-*Brahma Sūtra* teachers and the views attributed to them are given therein.

Notes

1. A free translation of:
इयं विसृष्टिर्यत आबभूव यदि वा दधे, यदि वा न दधे।
योऽस्याध्यक्षः परमे व्योमन्, सोऽङ्ग वेद यदि वा न वेद।।
— *ṚV*, 10.187.7 (नासदीय सूक्त)

2. जगद्व्यापारवर्जं प्रकरणात् असंनिहितत्त्वाच्च।
— *BrSū*, 4.4.17

3. अस्थास्यदेकरूपेण वपुषा चेन्महेश्वरः।
महेश्वरत्त्वं संवित्त्वं तदत्यक्षद् घटादिवत्।।
— *तन्त्रालोक*, III.100

4. तस्मात् सर्वज्ञत्वं, सर्वशक्तित्त्वं च सिद्धं निरङ्कुश-जगत्कर्तृत्वेन।
— *अणुभाष्य* on *BrSū*, 1-1.2

5. तत्र किं समवायि-निमित्तकर्तृ वा... यद्येकमेव स्यात् तदा क्रिया-ज्ञानशक्तयोर्निरतिशयत्त्वं भज्येत। मृदादि-साधारण्यं स्यात्। Later on *BrSū*, 1.1.3 Vallabhācārya says: अस्ति-भाति प्रियत्वेन सच्चिदानन्दरूपेण अन्वयत्वात्, नामरूपयोः कार्यत्वात् etc.
— *Ibid.*, on *BrSū*, 1.1.3

6. तदनन्यत्वमारम्भणशब्दादिभ्यः।
— *BrSū*, 2.114

7. यथा सोम्यैकेन मृत्पिण्डेन सर्वं मृन्मयं विज्ञातःस्यात्, वाचारम्भणं विकारो नामधेयं मृत्तिकेत्येव सत्यम्।
— *छान्दोग्य उपनिषद्*, 6.1.4

8. सर्व-वेदान्त-सारस्य सौरभास्वादमोदिनाम्।
आर्याणां शिवनिष्ठानां भाष्यमेतन्महानिधिः।।
— Introduction to *Brahma-Mīmāṁsā Bhāṣya*

9. वाड्.मनसि सम्पद्यते (*छान्दोग्य*, 6.8.6) इति वचनात् मनसा वाक् सम्पद्यते, *न तु तत्र लीयते।*

—*श्रीभाष्य* on *BrSū*, 4.2.1

(Karamarkara's Tramlation, p. 987)

10. तस्मादत्र वृत्त्युपसंहार विवक्षा।

वाग्वृत्तिः पूर्व मुपसे ह्रियते मनोवृत्तावविस्थितायाम् इत्यर्थः ।

— शारीरभाष्य on *BrSū*, 4.2.1 (8. 856)

11. वागादीनां मनसि न स्वरूपस्य उच्यते किन्तु वृत्तिलय एव।

ब्रह्ममीमांसा भाष्य, II, p. 451

12. G.V. Tagare, *Śaiva Darśan* (Marāṭhī), pp. 162-74.

13. शरीरमेव शरीरकम्, शरीरके भवः शारीरकः जीवः।

तभधिकृत्य कृतो ग्रन्थः शारीरकः।।

— *पञ्चपादिका*, p. 40

3

Pre-Brahma Sūtra Teachers

As we have seen that the *Brahma Sūtra* (*BrSū*) is an attempt to systematize the various strands of thoughts in the Upaniṣads, it reflects the systems of thought known at that time. Naturally Bādarāyaṇa quotes ancient teachers who entertained different views on important points of doctrines. Modern readers may not be interested in the topics regarding *Vaiśvānara* or the span-like size of the *ātman* or whether the priest or the *yajamāna* should perform the *japa* (muttering of *mantras*). But in those times, people regarded them as important topics for discussion. We find that Bādarāyaṇa records the viewpoints of those ancient (pre-*Brahma Sūtra*) teachers.

Contents of the BrSū.

The *Brahma Sūtra* has four chapters or *adhyāyas* each of which is divided into four *pādas* (parts), each *pāda* being subdivided into *adhikaraṇas* (sections, topics) consisting of *sūtras*. Each section deals with a specific point. If the section consists of more than one *sūtra*, generally the first *sūtra*(s) states an objection (*pūrva-pakṣa*) and the latter part of the section refutes the objection and states the *siddhānta*.

According to *Pūrva-Mīmāṁsā* every *adhikaraṇa* or section has five factors:

1. *Viṣaya* — subject-matter
2. *Viṣaya* — doubt or uncertainty
3. *Pūrva-pakṣa* — statement of objection

4. *Siddhānta* — established conclusion or the final decision
5. *Saṅgati* — connection between different sections

In spite of different philosophical views, commentators have normally preserved the arrangement of topics, the meaning of the *sūtras* to a great extent, references to the texts intended and *viṣaya-vākyas*.[1]

As stated above, the *BrSū* consists of four chapters:

1. *Samanvaya* — It tries to offer coherent interpretation of different texts of the Upaniṣads. The method of reconciliation has some social implications as well.
2. *Avirodha* consists of the refutation of the objections of rival schools (and criticism of their tenets), Sāṁkhyas, Jains, Buddhists, Pāñcarātras, etc. It shows the consistency and correctness of the views in the first chapter.
3. *Sādhanā* gives the exposition of the means for the realization of the *Brahman*.
4. *Phala* or Fruit of Knowledge is the topic of the fourth (and the last) chapter.

Pre-Brahma Sūtra Teachers

Bādarāyaṇa gives the following list of previous (pre-*Brahma Sūtra*) teachers. (For the sake of convenience, they are alphabetically arranged here). (1) Āśmarathya, (2) Ātreya, (3) Auḍulomi, (4) Bādarāyaṇa, (5) Bādari, (6) Jaimini, (7) Kārṣṇājini, (8) Kāśakṛtsna.

1. ĀŚMARATHYA

The name Āśmarathya is found in *Āśvalaẏana Śrauta Sūtra* and *Mīmāṁsā Sūtra* (6.5.16). Hence, he seems to be an expert in rituals and ritualistic Mīmāṁsā. Pāṇini (4.3.105) mention *Āśmaratha Kalpa* as a new ritualistic learning which shows that he lived earlier than Pāṇini.

The views of Āśmarathya are mentioned under two topics in the *BrSū*.

(1) *Vaiśvānara* is *Brahman* (1.2. 24-32).

(2) The self to be seen, heard, etc., is the highest self on account of the connection of the texts.

The first Sūtra

Abhivyakter ity āśmarathyah, 1.2.29 occurs in section of the first chapter. In this section, *sūtras* 1.2.24 to 1.2.27 show that the term *Vaiśvānara* does not imply gastric or abdominal fire. It is neither the Fire-god nor the gross element (*mahābhūta*) called Fire, *Vaiśvānara* is the *Para-Brahman.*

Āśmarathya opines that the *Chāndogya Upaniṣad* (5.18.1) mentioned that *Vaiśvānara* or the *Brahman* is measured by a span. Though the Supreme is transcendental of all measures, it manifests itself (*abhivyakti*) for its devotees in a limited form. The opinion is expressed in the *sūtra* which literally means:

> On account of manifestation (*abhivyakti*) (thinks) Āśmarathya.

Rāmānuja and Śrīkaṇṭha interpret the word *abhivyakti* as 'definiteness'.

Bādari (another pre-*BrSū* teacher) supports the view, stating that the Highest self said to be measured by a span since he is remembered (*anusmṛtaḥ*) by means of the mind located in the heart of span-length. Jaimini (another pre-*BrSū* teacher) says that is is appropriate to call the Highest self *pradeśa-mātra* (of the dimension of a span) and scriptures declares him to be so imagined (*sampatteḥ*) for the purpose of meditation (1.2.31).

Vallabhācārya interprets Āśmarathya's view in *BrSū* 1.2.29, as follows:

> The *Brahman* is formless. It is concealed by the screen (*javanikā*) of *māyā*. When *māyā* disappers, the *Brahman* manifests itself as Viṣṇu or *Puruṣa Vaiśvānara*. The *māyā* enveloped form of the *Brahman* is not real. The real form implied by Āśmarathya is *saccidānada-rūpa* (comprised of existence, consciousness and bliss).

Vallabhācārya firmly states that strong proof should be adduced to whatever view is expressed.[2]

The (Visible Self: The Great Self)

Āśmarathya holds that (the visible, audible) self is the Highest self. *BrSū*, 1.4.20 answers the doubt raised in the previous *sūtra* whether the *ātman* to be seen, heard, etc., mentioned in the *Bṛhadāraṇyaka Upaniṣad*[3] (4.5.6.) is the individual self or the Highest self. Āśmarathya, opines that the reference to the individual soul to be seen or heard indicates the proof of the statement (*pratijñā siddhi*). If the individual soul is different from the supreme soul, the former will not know the latter and the statement: 'though the knowledge of one thing, all things are known' will become invalid. There is non-difference betweeen the individual self and Supreme Self.

Bhāskara explains that the relations between the two (the individual Soul and the Supreme Soul) is like that between fire and the sparks emanating from the fire. It is the doctrine of *bhedābheda* (difference-cum-non-difference) which was taught in old Upaniṣads like *Bṛhadāraṇyaka* (2.1.20) and *Muṇḍaka*, (2.1.1). And this analogy of Fire-sparks relation is adopted by later Vedānta writers.

Thus, according to Bhāskara, the relation between individual soul and the Supreme Soul is *bhedābheda* (difference-cum-non-difference). It is neither absolutely different nor non-different from the *Brahman*, as it is like the sparks that emanate from the fire.

Auḍulomi (another pre-*BrSū*, teacher) teaches that the soul is altogether different from the *Brahman* up to the time of his final release, when it is merged into the *Brahman* (*BrSū*, 1.4.21). Thus, Auḍulomi suggests difference between the individual Soul and the *Brahman* in the state of bondage and non-difference in the *mokṣa* stage. Kāśakṛtsna (another pre-*BrSū*, teacher) regards the individual soul is absolutely non-different from the *Brahman* as the individual soul abides in (*avasthiteḥ*) in the Supreme (*BrSū*, 1.4.22).

Vallabhācārya quotes the above views of Āśmarathya, Auḍulomi, Kāśakṛtsna and comes to the conclusion that the doctrine of causality of *prakṛti* is not supported by Śruti. Only *Brahma-Vāda* is tenable.[4]

2. ĀTREYA

This sage Ātreya in *BrSū*, is different from Bhikṣu Ātreya of the fifth century AD who is mentioned in the *Caraka Saṁhitā*. Ātreya was a respectable scholar of the Veda and Vedic rituals as his name occurs in the *Mīmāṁsā Sūtra*, *Kātyāyana Śrauta Sūtra* and *Bodhāyana Gṛhya Sūtra*.

There is nothing philosophical about his doctrine. The problem is whether meditations (*sāma*-songs, etc.) connected with sacrificial acts are to be performed by the priest (employed for the sacrifice) or by the sacrificer (*yajamāna*). The problem is: who is the agent, the priest employed or the sacrificer (employer). Ātreya holds that the agentship of the act belongs to the sacrificer because he is the receiving the fruit of the sacrifice.[5]

But Auḍulomi differs. He says that the priest is paid for the act and as such he (the priest) must observe the meditations (because) they are the work of the priest.[6] Śaṅkara quotes the *Chāndogya Upaniṣad* (1.7.8) and holds that Auḍulomi is correct. The next *sūtra* states that this view is endorsed by Śrūti texts.

3. AUDULOMI

Audulomi was a respectable thinker of his age. In addition to his philosophical contribution, he seems to wield influence in the field of grammar as Patañjali mentions him in the *Mahābhāṣya* on Pāṇini 4.1.83.

Auḍulomi's view as against Ātreya's is discussed above. He is mentioned in *BrSū*, 1.4.21 about the relation of individual soul with the Supreme Soul (see above on Āśmarathya). He opines that the identification of the individual soul with the Supreme Soul is possible because when the individual soul 'rises' to depart from the body) he becomes one with the Supreme Soul.[7]

Thus, Auḍulomi holds that up to the time of final release (*mokṣa*), the soul is different from the *Brahman* but after that, he merges with the *Brahman* bereft of his name and form like rivers joining the sea.[8]

This *Bhedābheda-Vāda* of Auḍulomi is explained by Bhāskara and Vācaspati Miśra by quoting from *Pañcarātra Āgama*.[9]

> Up to Liberation, the individual self and the Supreme Self are different. But when liberated, there exists no distinction or a cause for distinction.
>
> — Bhāmati on 1.4.21

Śrīpati fully endorses the *Bhedābheda-Vāda*. Later the section on the state of the released soul in the *mukta* state, Auḍulomi believes[10] (*BrSū*,4.4.6).

> Solely as pure intelligence or consciousness (the soul manifests itself) as that being its self: Thus Auḍulomi thinks. This is opposed to Jaimiṇi's view in *BrSū*, 4.4.5. Jaimini thinks that the released soul's nature is like that of *Brahman*. It possesses qualities mentioned in *Chāndogya Upaniṣad*, 8.7.1. (The self is free from evil, old age, death, grief, hunger and thirst. There is such a freedom in all the world.)[11]

Bādarāyaṇa accepts Auḍulomi's view as against Jaimini's.

Vallabhācārya does not regard that there is any contradiction between the views of Jaimini and Auḍulomi as the soul's enjoyment is attributed to the volition (*saṅkalpa*) of the *Brahman*.

4. BĀDARĀYAṆA

Bādarāyaṇa is traditionally believed to be the author of the *Brahma Sūtra* (*BrSū*). Respectable Vedānta teachers like Madhva, Rāmānuja, Vallabha identify him with Veda-Vyāsa, the author of the *Mahābhārata* and the compiler of the Vedas. But the very fact that the Vedas and the *Mahābhārata* were already compiled before the *BrSū* shows that Bādarāyaṇa (the popularly believed author of *BrSū*) and Veda-Vyāsa are different persons. Some scholars believe that as the *BrSū* quotes some views as those of Bādarāyaṇa as if, he is the third person, Bādarāyaṇa cannot be the author of *BrSū*. It is, however, the practice of ancient Indian authors to mention their views in the third person as is done by Jaimini, Kauṭilya, Vātsyāyana (the author of *Kāma-Sūtra*). Winternitz suggests that the work is a compilation of scholars of Bādarāyaṇa's school and not the actual work of one author, viz. Bādarāyaṇa.

The references to Bādarāyaṇa in *BrSū* have been accepted as Siddhānta by commentators but the final verdict of the last redactor of *BrSū* does NOT necessarily accept these views as authoritative, though in majority of cases the redactor regards Bādarāyaṇa's views as authoritative.

As Bādarāyaṇa's views on every topic in *BrSū* are included in the present text, they are not separately listed here.

5. BĀDARI

Bādari seems to be well-versed in Vedic scholarship and rituals in general as his name as expert in Vedic ritual is mentioned in the *Mīmāṁsā Sūtra* (6.1.27), *Kātyāyana Śrauta Sūtra*. His views are quoted on the following topics:

a. *Vaiśvānara: Brahman: Extent*

The point under discussion is why the *Chāndogya Upaniṣad* (5.18) should teach that *Vaiśvānara* fire (i.e. the self or the Supreme Soul) should be worshipped as of being of a span in extent.[12] Āśmarathya explains that the Supreme Soul, though immeasurable, manifests Himself as being of a limited space for facilitating His worship (*BrSū,* 1.2.29). On this Rāmānuja and Śrīkaṇṭha say that the Lord assumes a definite form for facilitating the concentration of devotees. But Bādari explains (*BrSū,* 1.2.30) that this extent (space of one span) is presumed as if He is remembered in the mind. He is located in a span-sized heart.

Brahmasūtrakāra accepts Bādari's views.[13]

b. Soul's new embodiment: Nature of the new birth determind by *the clinging Karmas*

The point arose from the statement in the *Chāndogya Upaniṣad* (5.10.7) which says:

> Those of excellent (*ramaṇīya*) conduct get an excellent category of birth such as brāhmaṇa or kṣatriya but with bad (*kapūya*) conduct obtain a bad or contemptible birth like that of a cāṇḍala or a dog.[14]

Kārṣṇājini (a pre-*BrSū* teacher) thinks:[15]

> If it is said that on account of conduct (the assumption of residual *karma* is not necessary) we (Kārṣṇājini) say that it is not so (for the word *caraṇa* 'conduct' is used) to denote indirectly (the residual *karma*) — so thinks Kārṣṇājini. (*BrSū*, 3.1.9)

As *karma* is determined by good conduct, it (conduct) is not purposeless. It is *karma* and not conduct which is the seed of new birth.

But according to Bādari:[16]

> (Conduct means) good and evil *karmas* only (*eva*). There is no real difference between conduct (*caraṇa*) and *karma*. So residual *karma* is the cause of a new birth on the earth.

The author of *BrSū* accepts this view.

c. *Speculation: Post-death state of the soul*

The topic begins with Bādari's assertion:

> To the *kārya Brahman* (*saguṇa Brahman* or *apara Brahman*) the souls are led, on account of the possibility of being the goal (*gatyupa-patteḥ*).[17]

Bādari means to say that by *kārya*, *saguṇa* or *apara Brahman* is implied the possibility of the act of going, if the hypothesis of *Brahmaloka* and the soul's journey through the moon, etc., is presumed. As the *Brahman* is a cause or *nirguṇa Brahman* is all-pervading and is the inner-soul (*antarātman*) of all, the hypothesis of 'going to' is untenable.

Śaṅkara accepts this view in the conclusion of his commentary on this *sūtra*.[18]

Rāmānuja (as interpreted by Karmarkar) on this *sūtra*:

> Not, indeed, in the case of the worshipper of the Highest *Brahman* which is perfect all around, omniscient, all-pervading, the *ātman* of all, is appropriate in going to another region to attain to it (*para-Brahman*).[19]

Rāmānuja does not believe in complete merger of the soul with the *Brahman.*

d. *Released Souls: Embodied or Bodyless*

The possession of Will means the released soul has a mind. But Bādari says he has not the organs or the body (*abhāvam*) as it is said in the scriptures (*Chāndogya Upaniṣad*, 8.12.5) the mind is his divine eye wherewith he rejoices:

manasā eva etān kāmān paśyan ramate
— *Chāndogya Upaniṣad*, 8.12.5

Radhakrishnan says that such a soul possesses mind only and not the body (*Brahma Sūtra*, p. 556). In the Ultimate stage of liberation the (bodyless) soul returns to this natural stage (Brahmahood).

Vallabhācārya: According to *puṣṭi-mārga* one gets a body from God. Therewith the soul enjoys the bliss of *bhajana* (Devotion).

6. JAIMINI

Jaimini was one of the the greatest *ācāryas* of the pre-*BrSū* period. A branch of *Sāmaveda*, a *Brāhmaṇa* work, and an Upaniṣad and *Gṛhya Sūtra* are associated with his name. The tradition, however, confirms that he wrote the following works:

(1) (*Pūrva*) *Mīmāṁsā Sūtra*, (2) *Devatākāṇḍa* and (3) *Śārīraka Sūtra.*

Upavarṣa and Bodhāyana, wrote commentaries on his *Mīmāṁsā Sūtra* but they are superseded by Śabarasvāmin who, in his Bhāṣya, mentions the names of these precursors. Sureśvara believes that Jaimini wrote a *Śārīrika Sūtra* and quotes the first two *sūtras* found in the extant *BrSū*, though Jaimini's *Brahma Sūtra* has not come down to us.

The *BrSū* quotes Jaimini at the following places: 1.2.28, 1.2.31, 1.3.31, 1.4.18, 3.2.40, 3.4.2, 3.4.18, 3.4.40, 4.3.12, 4.4.5, and 4.4.11.

The name of the topic and Jaimini's opinion on each of them is as follows:

BrSū, 1.2.28

The topic is whether Vaiśvānara in *Chāndogya Upaniṣad*, (V.1.18) means *Brahman*,Jaimini says "There is no contradiction even if the Supreme Self is taken as the object to worship (as Vaisvānara) directly.[20]

BrSū, 1.2.31: The dimension of God — a span

Jaimini: (God is said to be a span in length) on account of the imaginative identification. What Jaimini means "it is proper to call the Supreme Self (*pradeśa mātra*) of the length of a span for the purpose of meditation". Hence *Chāndogya's* (5.11-18) statement.[21]

BrSū, 1.3.31

The topic is about the eligibility of gods for the knowledge of the *Brahman*. Jaimini says: "On account of the impossibility (of the gods having a right to the knowledge of) the honey and the rest, (gods) are not eligible because they cannot themselves become the object of their own meditation.[22]

BrSū, 1-4-18: Topic: Causality of the Brahman

According to *Kauṣītakī Upaniṣad* (4.19) the Maker (Creator) of the world alone should be known. But it is the individual Soul, *prāṇa* (chief vital breath or the Supeme Soul) that is to be so known. Jaimini says: Even if we presume that it is a reference to individual soul, it is only to indicate the knowledge of the *Brahman*. The self exists beyond (life principle and the *jīva* (individual Soul).[23]

3.2.40

The topic is whether the merits or demerits (for one's *karmas*) conferred by God or they are the automatic results of the *karmas* of the person concerned.

Jaimini holds that religious merits (is what brings about the fruits of *karmas*). The scriptural injunctions such as *svargakāmo yajeta* gives no scope to an outside agent like God to impart the fruit.[24] He takes his stand on the *apūrva* theory in *Pūrva Mīmāṁsā Sūtra*, 2.1.5. Bādarāyaṇa refutes it in the next *Sūtra* (*BrSū,* 3.2.41).

3.4.2: Topic: The knowledge of Brahman is independent and not subordinate to Karma

In the previous *sūtra* (3.4.1) of Bādarāyaṇa on the srtrength of *Chāndogya Upaniṣad* (7.1.3), states that the knowledge of *Brahman* leads to liberation and is not a part of sacrificial *karmas*. As against this, Jaimini says:[25] The Self is in a supplementary position to *karma* (*śeṣatvāt*). Hence (the statement as to the fruits of knowledge of the Self) are mere praise of the Agent even as in other cases. In plain words, for Jaimini the knowledge of the Self has no independent fruit of its own because the knowledge of the self as the agent in all actions stands in subordinate relation to action (ritual). Jaimini is rather biased to ritualitic *karmas*.

3.4.18: Topic: Prescription of only Brahmavidyā in Saṁsāra

Regarding preservation of Knowledge (*Brahmavidyā*) in the state of *saṁsāra*, Jaimini opposes *saṁnyāsa*, for Upaniṣads like the *Chāndogya*, 2.23.1, only refer to *saṁnyāsa* and there is no injunction (to take it). Other texts condemn it.[26]

3.4.40: Topic: Non-reversion from Saṁnyāsa to the previous stage

Jaimini says that one who has entered the *saṁnyāsa* stage cannot go back to the previous stages of life, for the texts (Śrutis) do not speak of reversion but only of ascent to the higher stages of life.[27]

4.3.12: Topic: The Devayāna Path leads to Saguṇa Brahma

Souls are led to the highest (*Brahman*). When two meanings are possible, the higher one should be preferred.[28] *Brahman* can mean the higher and lower. Jaimini says that the higher meaning should be adopted vide *Chāndogya Upaniṣad*, 4.15.5.

4.4.5: The Topic: Characteristics of the released Soul

Jaimini asserts that (the released soul exists) as possessed of the nature of the *Brahman* as mentioned in the *Chāndogya Upaniṣad* (8.7.1).

Jaimini thinks that the released soul is like the *Brahman* in nature.[29] It possesses qualities mentioned in the *Chāndogya Upaniṣad* (8.7.1).

> The soul which is free from evil, free from old age, free from death, free from grief, free from hunger and thirst, whose desire is real, whose thought is real. For such there is freedom in all the world.

4.4.11: The Topic: Released souls — embodied or disembodied

Released souls are embodied or disembodied according to their will. Jaimini thinks that there is presence of the body and sense-organs because the scriptures desire capacity to asssume diverse forms.[30]

Whatever be the impressions carried by the expression of diverse views of Jaimini, he, though author of the *Pūrva Mīmāṁsā*, was also deepely studied in Upaniṣads or Vedānta (*Uttara-Mīmāṁsā*).

7. KĀRṢṆĀJINI

Kārṣṇājini is mentioned in *Mīmāṁsā Sūtra* (4.3.17) and *Kātyāyana Śrauta Sūtra*. He seems to be an expert in ritual.

The topic is the determination of new birth according to *karma*s.

Kārṣṇājini says: If it be said that depending upon conduct (in this world one attains various births) it is not so. The word conduct (*caraṇa*) in the *BrSū* (III.1.9) refers to the remainder of the *karma*. The man who does not perform good conduct cannot obtain food reward even if he does carry out the rituals. This idea is confirmed later in *Vasiṣtha Smṛti* (6.3) which says "The Vedas do not purify the man who is devoid of good conduct and good conduct determines *karma* and is therefore not purposeless." In *BrSū,* III.1.11 Bādari clarifies 'there is no difference between conduct or *caraṇa* and *karma*'.

Kaśa Kṛtsna or Kāśakṛtsni

There are two spellings of this *ācārya*'s name — Kāśakṛtsna and Kāśakṛtsni but they are the names of the same teacher. Kāśakṛtsna was a Vedic scholar. Bhaṭṭa Bhāskara Miśra mentions him along with Yāska. His name occurs in *Baudhāyana Gṛhya Sūtra. The Kātyāyana*

Śrauta Sūtra mentions him along with ancient teachers like Bādari and Kārṣṇājini. Patañjali mentions him as a Mīmāṁsā writer and the students of that Mīmāṁsā were called *Kāśakṛtsnas*, a form accepted as ancient one and therefore, an accepted form in *Kāśikā* (on Pāṇini 4.3.3.01). Helarāja, a commentator on Bhartṛhari's *Vākyapadīya* attributes a grammatical work to Kāśakṛtsna.

The *BrSū* knows him as a philosopher and accepts his views on the relation between the individual self and the Supreme Soul.

Before accepting Kāśakṛtsna's view as Siddhānta *BrSū* quoted the views of Āśmarathya, and Auḍulomi. By the term *avasthiteḥ* in the *sūtra* 1.4.22, Kāśakṛtsna means the relation between the individual self and the Supreme Self are not of complete non-difference but the individual self is a part of (*aṁśa*), i.e. a constitutent of the Higher Self.[31] For in *BrSū*, 2.3.43 '*aṁśo nānā-vyapadeśat,* etc.' suggests that the soul is a part of the *Brahman*, as the sparks are of fire. In the Śruti there are statements showing difference and non-difference in the Soul and the *Brahman* (*Bhedābheda*) and that the individual self is only an *aṁśa*, a constitutent part of the *Brahman*.

The *Bhedābheda-Vāda* of Kāśakṛtsna influenced later *ācārya*s like Bhāskara and Vallabha.

The contribution of the *Brahma Sūtrapūrva* teachers is generally passed over in histories of Indian philosophy. As they have influenced later philosophers liked Bhāskara, Vallabha and others, their specific contribution is noted here.

Notes

1. Radhakrishnan — *The Brahma Sūtra*, Introduction, pp. 23-24.
2. तस्मात् प्रमाणमेवानुवर्तव्यम्। न युक्तिः। शब्दबल-विचार एव युक्तः।
   — AB on *BrSū,* 1.2.32, Vol. II, p. 600
3. आत्मा वा अरे द्रष्टव्यः, श्रोतव्यो निदिध्या सितव्यः . . . . आत्मनि खल्वरे दृष्टे, श्रुत्ते, मते, विज्ञात इद्ंःसर्वं विज्ञातं भवति।
   — बृहदारण्यक उपनिषद, 4.5.6
4. See The concluding portion of AB on *BrSū,* 1.4.23 Vallabhācārya's final conclusion: श्रुतिसामर्थ्यं प्रमाणमित्युक्तम्। तस्माद् ब्रह्म एव समवायकारणं न प्रकृतिः।
   — AB on *BrSū,* 1.4.23 Vol. II. pp. 957-75

5. स्वामिनः फलश्रुतेरित्याभेदः।

— *BrSū*, 3.4.44

6. आर्त्विज्यम् इति औडुलोमिः। तस्मै हि परिक्रीयते।

— *BrSū*, 3.4.45

7. उत्क्रमिष्यत एवं भावादित्यौडुलोमिः।

— *BrSū*, 1.4.21

8. Major commentaries on the *BrSū* on this *sūtra* quote the following verse in support of their view:

यथा नद्यः स्यन्दमानाः समुद्रेऽस्तं गच्छन्ति नामरूपे विहाय।

तथा विद्वान् नामरूपाद वियुक्तः परात्परं पुरुषमुपैति दिव्यम्।।

9. आमुक्तेर्भेद एव स्याज्जीवस्य च परस्य च।

मुक्तस्य तु न भेदोऽस्ति देहहेतोरभावतः।।

— *पाञ्चरात्र* quoted in *भामनी*, 1.4.21

10. चितितन्मात्रेण तदात्मकत्वाद् इति औडुलोमिः।

— *BrSū*, 4.4.6

11. य आत्माऽपहतपाप्मा विजरो विमृत्युर्विशोकोऽन्वेष्टव्यः।

— *छान्दोग्य उपनिषद*, 8.7.1

12. एते वै खलु . . . . यस्त्वेतं एवं प्रादेशमात्रमभिविमानमात्मानं वैश्वानरमुपास्ते स सर्वेषु लोकेषु सर्वेषु भूतेषु सर्वेष्वात्मस्वनमत्ति।

— *छान्दोग्य उपनिषद*, 5.18.1

13. अनुस्मृतेर्बादरिः।

— *BrSū*, 1.2.30

14. तद् य इह रमणीय-चरणा अभ्याशो ह यत्ते रमणीयां योनिमापद्येरन्। . . . . . अथ य कपूय-चरणा (of bad conduct) अभ्याशो ह यत्ते कपूयां (low) योनिमापद्येरन्।

— *छान्दोग्य उपनिषद*, 5.10.7

15. चरणादिति चेत्, न, उपलक्षणार्थेति कार्ष्णाजिनिः।

— *BrSū*, 3.1.9

16. सुकृत-दुष्कृते एवेति तु बादरिः।

— *BrSū*, 3.1.11

17. कार्यं बादरिरस्य गत्युपपत्तेः।

— *BrSū*, 4.3.7

18. अस्य हि कार्यब्रह्मणो गन्तव्यत्वमुपपद्यते, प्रदेशवत्त्वात्। न तु परस्मिन् ब्रह्मणि गन्तृत्वं गन्तव्यत्वं गतिर्वा न कल्पते।

— Śaṅkara on *BrSū*,4.3.7, p. 880

19. न हि परिपूर्णं सर्वज्ञं सर्वगतं सर्वात्मीभूतं परब्रह्मोपासीनस्य तत्प्राप्तये देशान्तरगतिरुपपद्यते, प्राप्तत्वादेव।

— Rāmānuja on *Ibid.*, Vol. III, p. 1026

20. साक्षादप्यविरोधं जैमिनिः।

— *BrSū,* 1.2.28

21. सम्पत्तेरिति जैमिनिस्तथा हि दर्शयति।

— *BrSū,* 1.2.31

22. मध्वादिष्वसम्भवादनधिकारं जैमिनिः।

— *BrSū,* 1.3.31

23. अन्यार्थं तु जैमिनिः प्रश्नव्याख्यानाभ्यामपि चैवमेके।

— *BrSū,* 1.4.18

24. धर्मं जैमिनिरत एव।

— *BrSū,* 3.2.40

25. शेषत्वात् पुरुषार्थवादो यथान्येष्विति जैमिनिः।

— *BrSū,* 3.4.2

26. परामर्शं जैमिनिरचोदना चापवदति हि।

— *BrSū,* 3.4.18

27. तद्भूतस्य तु नातद्भावः, जैमिनेरपि नियमात् तद्रूपाभावेभ्यः।

— *BrSū,* 3.4.40

28. परं जैमिनिर्मुख्यत्वात्।

— *BrSū,* 4.3.12

29. ब्राह्मेण जैमिनिरुपन्यासादिभ्यः।

— *BrSū,* 4.4.5

30. भावं जैमिनिर्विकल्पामननात्।

— *BrSū,* 4.4.11

31. अवस्थितेरिति काशकृत्स्नः।

— *BrSū,* 1.4.22

4

Pre-Vallabha Vedānta Thought

We have seen that the *Brahma Sūtras* (*BrSū*) were called the *Vedānta Sūtra*, as they dealt with the topics in the Upaniṣads which formed the last part of the Vedic literature, the other previous parts being *Saṁhitā*, *Brāhmaṇa* and *Āraṇyakas*. In the Upaniṣads, there were two main thought-currents — one affirming the identity of the *Brahman*, the individual soul and the world, and the other which distinguished between them *inter se*. Some teachers attempted to reconcile these different views. Bādarāyaṇa was the last author and probably a successful one in synthesizing them. He arranged the different Upaniṣadic views under separate sections or titles and presented them in laconic but intelligible *sūtras*. As some of the views stated to be those of Bādarāyaṇa were not accepted as *siddhānta* in the *BrSū*, the redactor of the present *BrSū* must be different than Bādarāyaṇa. Bādarāyaṇa, however, deserves the credit of presenting a coherent view of those bygone philosophical debates.

As a background of the philosophical contribution of Vallabhācārya, it is necessary to take a bird's-eye view of the philosophical debate that took place before Vallabhācārya. In this debate, the pattern of thought about the relation of God, man and the world was more important than the designation of the God as Śiva, Viṣṇu, Śakti, etc. Hence, though Vallabhācārya was a Vaiṣṇava, contribution of Vaiṣṇava and non-Vaiṣṇava *ācāryas* before Vallabhācārya are briefly noted.

Gauḍapāda

The outstanding Vedāntic teacher before Śaṅkara was his teacher's teacher, Gauḍapāda. Little historical information about him is available. Though a number of works are attributed to him, the *Māṇḍūkya Kārikā* is the only work that is accepted as his contribution to Vedānta. Some *kārikās* from that work are quoted as *pūrva-pakṣa* by the Buddhist philosopher Bhāvaviveka or Bhavya[1] (*circa* AD 490-520). It leads us to fix the probable date of Gauḍapāda and that of Śaṅkarācārya.

As Gauḍapāda wrote his *kārikās* earlier than Bhavya's work, Gauḍapāda's date is automatically confirmed. And also the date of the pupil's (Govinda Yati) pupil, viz., Śaṅkara. A generation is regarded as a period of 30 years. So Śaṅkara lived 60 years after Gauḍapāda in *circa* AD 550 (AD 490 + 60). I hope scholars will reconsider the erroneous date of Śaṅkara, viz., AD 788. As is well-known, Brāhmaṇism and Buddhism shared the philosophic thoughts of Upaniṣads and used common terms, sometimes with different implications. Hence some scholars like S.N. Dasgupta seem to regard Gauḍapāda a Buddhist, but other scholars like T.M.P. Mahadevan (*Gauḍapāda, A Study in Advaita Vedānta*, Madras, 1952), S. Roy (*Heritage of Śaṅkara*, Allahabad, 1968) have shown that Gauḍapāda's *Advaita* and Nāgārjuna's *Advaya* are not the same and the apparent similarities in *kārikās* of Gauḍapāda and Nāgārjuna are deceptive. Lastly the very fact that the Buddhist philosopher Bhavya quotes Gauḍapāda as *pūrva-pakṣa* is enough to show that he (Gauḍapāda) is not a Buddhist. Gauḍapāda is credited to have written a number of works such as the commentary on *Sāṁkhya Kārikās*, but the only authentic work generally accepted as such is his *Māṇḍūkya Kārikās*.

This work is divided into four parts or sections:

1. *Āgama*: This explains the text of the *Māṇḍūkya Upaniṣad*. He shows that his views have the sanction of the Śruti and are reinforced by reason.

2. *Vaitathya*: It shows the phenomenal nature of the world.

3. This establishes the Advaita theory.

4. *Alāte-Śānti* (Extinguishing the circle of a fire-brand).

When a torch or a stick burning at the end is whirled in a circle, it gives the illusion of a circle of fire, so is the multiplicity of the world and proves the Advaitic position about the reality of the Soul.

To state briefly:

Gauḍapāda holds:

(1) The doctrine of *Ajāti*

Nothing comes into being (*Māṇḍūkya Kārikā*, IV-19)

(2) All the appearances (*dharmas*) are like the Vacuous sky (*gaganopama*)

(3) Duality is distinction imposed on the non-dual (*advaita*) by *māyā*.

Whatever has a beginning has an end, hence unreal. The *Brahman* is *kūṭastha* (unchanging). Causality is a false notion. Things are produced apparently and not in reality.

Gauḍapāda, the staunch exponent of the *Advaita Vedānta* says that the *Advaita Vedānta* (*Asparśa Yoga*) is pleasing to all and hostile to none.[2]

Śaṅkara

Though there is considerable similarity in the views of the Śaiva and Vaiṣṇava Monists, Śaiva and Vaiṣṇava Dualists, etc., they did not inter-borrow as it is the practice in India to quote only from one's own *pūrva sūris* (preceding authors) and NOT from those from the other alien schools. Even in telling a common narrative such as the story of Rāma, Śvetāmbara Jain authors mention or refer to their *pūrva sūris* and not to Digambara writers and *vice-versa*.

Like Śaiva philosophers, Śaṅkara probed mainly problems relating *to the following:*

(i) The Ultimare Reality

(ii) The Individual Soul

(iii) The Phenomenal World

THE ULTIMATE REALITY

According to Śaṅkara, the *Brahman* is the Ultimare Reality (*brahma satyam*). It is one, non-dual. It is *sat* (the Reality, existence), *cit* (pure consciousness) and *ānanda* (bliss). *Sat-cit-ānanda* constitute the very nature of the *Brahman* and *not* its qualities. The *Brahman* is both immanent and transcendent to the phenomenal world. Hence, Upaniṣads hold that the Absolute can be described by the words: Not this', 'Not that' (*neti, neti*) and by the negatively worded epithets *nirguṇa, nirākāra*, etc. Some *ācāryas* interpret the first as devoid of the qualities of *prakṛti,* viz., *sattva, rajas, tamas*; some, as devoid of unacceptable qualities (*heya-guṇas*). Some raise objection to the term *nirākāra* as saints or mystics visualize in their meditation innumerable forms of the Lord. Does *nirākāra* mean 'too innumerable to be counted or described'? About the *Brahman*, Śaṅkara adopts the Upaniṣadic view that one teaches it without speaking (*avacanena eva anubhavan uvāca*) as the *Brahman* is not only incomprehensible but also indescribable. The Brāhmaṇical *Avadhūta Gītā* states that the *Brahman* is beyond both Dvaita and Advaita.[3] The great Buddhist teacher Nāgārjuna seems to have reached to a similar conclusion about the nature of reality (see the *Mādhyamaka Kārikās* quoted in the Notes).[4]

The Date

As I have shown above, that due to Gauḍapāda' precedence in time, to the Buddhist philosopher Bhavya or Bhāvaviveka (AD 490-520), Śaṅkara should be located in the sixth century AD and not in the eighth century (AD 788) as is presumed by modern scholars.

After Gauḍapāda, Śaṅkara is the earliest Vaiṣṇava scholar who set the Monist (Advaita) school on solid foundations. I call Śaṅkara a Vaiṣṇava as his spiritual genealogy (*guru-paramparā*) starts from Viṣṇu.

There is another view which regards a person Vaiṣṇava who considers Viṣṇu as the Supreme Reality and a Śaiva who regards Śiva as the highest reality. As Viṣṇu and Śiva are the names of the same Supreme Reality, the *para-Brahman*, there is no need to emphasize differences such as Śaiva and Vaiṣṇava.

It is interesting to note that all great Vaiṣṇava teachers — Śaṅkara, Rāmānuja, Madhva, Vallabha hail from, the Dravidian-speaking south. Like Śaivite teachers, these Vaiṣṇava teachers have established their particular philosophical school (e.g., Monism, Dualism, etc.) while probing the main problems about the nature, relations, etc., of (i) the Ultimate Reality, (ii) The individual soul, (iii) The phenomenal world.

Śaṅkara's views about the nature, etc., of the Ultimate Reality are noted above.

THE INDIVIDUAL SOUL

About 'Individual Soul', Śaṅkara is firmly of the opinion that the individual soul (*jīva*) is the *Brahman* and is not different from it.[5]

THE PHENOMENAL WORLD

About the phenomenal world, Śaṅkara uses two terms: (i) *Māyā* and (ii) *Vivarta*. I am only stating Śaṅkara's views. Śaṅkara never calls himself *māyā-vādin*. He calls himself *aupaniṣada* and his doctrine as *aupaniṣada darśana* Vide His *Bhāṣya* on *BrSū*, II.2.10 and II.1.9

Māyā[6]

In Śaṅkara's writings, the term *māyā* denotes the following:

(1) The phenomenal character of the world.

(2) The incomprehensibility of the relation between the Ultimate Reality (*Brahman*) and the world of Plurality.

(3) The *Brahman* as the cause of the world as it (world) rests on the *Brahman*.

(4) The Principle which is assumed to account for the appearance of the *Brahman* as the world.

(5) If the concept of the empirical world is logically analysed, one arrives at the concept of *Iśvara* who has the power of self-expression. This power or Energy is called *māyā*.

Śaṅkara's concepts of *māyā* may be compared with the *māyā* concept of the Buddhist philosopher Nāgārjuna. He regards the concepts of origination, existence and annihilation of the nature of *māyā*, dreams or fairy castles in the heaven.[7]

As Śaṅkara is a refuter of Nāgārjuna's *śūnyavāda*, he should not be accused as a borrower from Nāgārjuna.

Śaivas had no need for such a complicated theory, as Para-Śiva (the Supreme Reality) has powers of knowledge (*prakāśa*) and Creativity (*vimarśa*). Śiva can create, maintain and destroy anything by his sheer Will Power without any material (*upādāna*) and instrument — a doctrine which reminds us of Vallabhācārya's concept of *Para-Brahman*.

Vivarta

Vivarta is 'apparent modification', explains Svāmī Vīreśvarānanda in his introduction to *Brahma Sūtra-Śrībhāṣya* (pp. lxxiv or 74):

> There is a view current that Vedānta Sūtras propound a theistic philosophy whatever be the nature of it and never Śaṅkara's Monism.

This view is not justified due to the fact that very many *Brahma Sūtras* . . . clearly point to *vivarta-vāda*

In the first *sūtra* (*BrSū*, 1.1.1) knowledge is intuitive knowledge attained through hearing (*śravaṇa*), reasoning (*manana*) and meditation (*nididhyāsana*) that leads to such knowledge which destroys the ignorance about *Brahman*, resulting in release (from *saṁsāra*). So, importance given to ***bhakti*** and grace by theistic commentators does not seem to be justified. Many *sūtras* clearly point to *vivarta-vāda* (e.g., *BrSū*, 1.4.23, II.1.14.20, II.3.50, III.2.18). The last two show that the author of *BrSū*) must have had *vivarta-vāda* (apparent modification) and *not pariṇāma-vāda* (actual modification) in view.

The fact is, Upaniṣads do not teach any particular doctrine. The doctrines expressed (as their contexts show) are for different levels.

In the introduction to *BrSū* Radhakrishnan says:

> Even according to Śaṅkara *The World is not non-existent*. *Brahman* with its *māyā* power is the cause of the world. The world has a relative empirical existence.

Śaṅkara, the theist, believes in personal God and describes the different attributes of the deity, be it Viṣṇu, Śiva or Śakti. His *stotras*, the outpouring of the heart of an ardent devotee, are recited everyday by many people. Acceptance of *saguṇa* or *apara Brahman* is the ground reality. The aspirants are taken step by step to the Ultimate truth from Dualism to qualified Monism and finally to Monism where they realize their identity with the *Brahman*.

Vallabhācārya's View

Vallabhācārya's views regarding the Supreme Reality Kṛṣṇa, the individual soul and the world are discussed in the following chapters in details, it will not be out of place to show the differences between Śaṅkara and Vallabha as both of them are bracketed as Monists. According to Vallabhācārya:

1. The *Brahman* is attributeless and yet possess all non-material (or *prakaṭa*) auspicious qualities.
2. In the *Brahman* all contradictions are resolved (*paraspara-viruddha-guṇāśraya*).
3. It is essentially *sat* (Existence), *cit* (Consciousness) and *ānanda* (Bliss) and has no connection with *māyā*.
4. The world is neither illusory nor is different from the Brahmā. The relation between the Brahmā and the world is one of identity (*sarvam khalu idam brahma*).
5. Both sentient and insentient beings are *Brahman* in essence but in the sentient, Bliss aspect of the *Brahman* is withheld and in the non-sentient, knowledge or consciousness and bliss are withheld. When these aspects which are withheld appear in them, they become one with the *Brahman*. It is especially the bliss-aspect by gaining which they become identical with the Brahmā.

Bhāskara (AD 1000)

Bhāskara strongly refutes Śaṅkara's *māyā-vāda*. He asserts that the *māyā-vāda* is the brain-child of Śaṅkara and has no basis in the Śruti.

Those who adopt *māyā-vāda* are Buddhists[8] — a baseless criticism as shown in the previous section. The *Brahman* is the Supreme Reality. It is both material and efficient cause of the Universe. The *Brahman* has two forms.[9]

(i) *Kāraṇa rūpa* (Causal) and

(ii) *Kārya rūpa* (the Effect)

The causal form of the *Brahman* is the original, while the effect form is due to *upādhis* (limiting adjuncts) and is, therefore, adventitious (*āgantuka*) *yet* real. The difference between the two is that the *Brahman* as the cause, is eternal forever, while the effect — *Brahman* is real but temporary (*anitya*). In the causal state the *Brahman* and the world are identical but in the effect stage, the *Brahman* and the Universe are different.

The *Brahman* is Pure Being (*sat-lakṣaṇa*), Pure Knowledge, omniscient, omnipotent. The *Brahman* is the essence of the Universe but *not vice-versa.*

Bhāskara rejects the Pāñcarātra theory of four *vyūhas*. He regards Upavarṣācārya as the founder of the school (*saṁpradāya — pravartaka*) and advises the performance of duties laid down in the *Pūrva-Mīmāṁsā* necessary before the study of the *BrSū*. Mere knowledge of scriptures is not enough for *mukti*. He advocates 'Coordination of *karma* and Knowledge' (*karma-jñāna-samuccaya*). He is propagator of *bhedābheda* and as such is a follower of Āśmarathya.

Rāmānuja (AD 1017-1127)

Rāmānuja is the chief exponent of Viśiṣṭādvaita philosophy. Radhakrishnan points out that 'qualified non-dualism' is not the correct rendering of the term *viśiṣṭādvaita*. It is *viśiṣṭasya advaita*, the non-dualism of the differences. It holds the unity of the conscious (*cit*) and the non-conscious, unintelligent (*acit*) with and in God whose body they constitute.

Radhakrishnan believes that the word *brahma-sūtra* in the *Bhagavad Gītā* (13-4)[10] supports the view that Bādarāyaṇa seems to be a theist rather than an absolutist.[11]

Rāmānuja's *magnum opus* is his monumental commentary *Śrī Bhāṣya* on the *BrSū*. His philosophy is influenced by the Bhāgavata doctrine, the *bhakti* cult of Aḷwārs (Vaiṣṇavaite Tamil saints). He synthesizes the old Aḷwār *prabandhas* with the theistic portion of old Upaniṣads, the Bhāgavata, the Pāñcarātra Āgamas as approved by *BrSū*, 2.2.41 and 42.

According to Rāmānuja, the Supreme Reality, the all-embracing Being called the *Brahman* is the mightiest Self. He is free from impurities and is endowed with auspicious qualities. He is omniscient and merciful. He is not *nirviśeṣa* (attributesless) as believed by Śaṅkara, Rāmānuja regards the *Brahman*, *Īśvara*, Nārāyaṇa and Viṣṇu identical. He postulates the *Brahman* qualified by the world of sentient (*cit*) and non-sentient (*acit*) as its body under all conditions, viz., *kāraṇa* and *kārya* (causal and an effect). Svāmī Vīreśvarānanda sums up the substance of the *Śrī Bhāsya* as follows:

> The substance of the *Śrī Bhāṣya* may be stated in four synoptic propositions:
>
> (1) It is a reasoned and critical reconstruction of the philosophy of Upaniṣads with due appropriation of other sources of knowledge such as perception and inference and the supplementary scriptures.
>
> (2) The reconstruction presents Ultimate Reality, *Brahman*, the Supreme spirit, as the transcendent repository of all perfections and as holding as its own embodiment the totality of finite existence, sentient and insentient.
>
> (3) The pathway to the final good of life is the blissful communion with the *Brahman* by way of devout and loving contemplation named *bhakti*, facilitated by a life of virtue and founded on assumed philosophical understanding.
>
> (4) The end attained through that means is the eternal experience of *Brahman*, with all the plentitude and eternity which only that experience can bring to the

individual personality. It is the Supreme ecstasy of *life in God*.[12]

The importance of the *Śrī Bhāṣya* lies in the amplitude of its substantiation of these fundamentals.

The following special concepts of Rāmānuja are worth noting:

(1) Rāmānuja interprets the famous *mahā-vākya 'tat tvam asi'* (That thou art) as oneness (with *Brahman*) without losing the distinctive characteristics denoted by the two words — *that* and *thou*.

(2) In the *mokṣa* stage, the soul enjoys its individuality. He participates in the qualities of *Īśvara* except the creation and control of the world. *Vedānta Deśika*, however, thinks *mukti* (*mokṣa*) is servitude to God.

(3) The way of *mokṣa* is *bhakti* and *prapatti* (complete surrender to the will of God).

Rāmānuja had such a broad outlook that he admitted into the Vaiṣṇava fold Jains, Buddhists, śūdras and even untouchables.[13] In a way Rāmānuja was a source of inspiration to later saints like Rāmānanda, Kabīr and others.

Madhva (AD 1238)

Next to Rāmānuja, Madhva made an important contribution to Indian philosophy — the establishement of Dualism or rather Dualistic Pluralism. Madhva deserves special attention as Vallabhācārya's teachers were followers of Madhva. Madhva refuted Śaṅkara's non-dualism (*Advaita*) and established the reality of the Personal God, Plurality of the world and the difference between individual souls and the *Brahman*. The *Brahman* is the only independent existence and Knowledge in essence. It is called 'indescribable' or 'unknowable' as it cannot be fully described or known. The *Brahman* is not associated with *guṇas* (*sattva*, *rajas* and *tamas*) of *prakṛti* and is hence called *nirguṇa* (quality-less).

Though Brahmā's infinite personality is beyond our comprehension, for His devotees He manifests Himself in finite from which is *not* material. Matter (*prakṛti*) is real and eternal but dependent on the *Brahman*. It undergoes modifications at the Will ofhe *Brahman* which is only an efficient cause. The *Brahman* is sentient and cannot be the creator of an insentient world.

Like other schools of Indian Philosophy, Madhva holds that the soul's are eternal (not created by the *Brahman*). They depend on the Lord who guides them to *mokṣa* — a positive blissful stage in which the soul does not lose his independent individuality. Madhva advocates the semitic doctrine of eternal hell to the wicked.[14]

In a period dominated by great advocates of Śaṅkara's theory of non-dualism, the credit of repudiating that doctrine, establishment of the reality of a Personal God, of Plurality of the world and difference between the *Brahman* and the souls, goes to Madhva (though he was an ascetic of Śaṅkara school) and to his followers like Jayatīrtha.

There have been great teachers like Yādava Prakāśa, Nimbārka and others before Vallabha. It will, however, require a separate book to trace in full the evolution of philosophical thought before Vallabha. As this is a small compendium of Vallabhācārya's *Brahma-Vāda*, I have limited myself to the main tenets of four prominent teachers, viz., Śaṅkara, Bhāskara, Rāmānuja and Madhva. These teachers are regarded as the most prominent exponents (though not founders) of the main schools of Veda-based) Indian Philosophy, viz., Monism (*advaita*), difference-cum-non-difference (*bhedābheda*), Qualified Monism (*viśiṣṭādvaita*) and Dualism or Pluralistic Dualism (*dvaita*).

It is on such a background that Vallabhācārya established his theory of *Śudhādvaita* or *Brahma-vāda*. What follows is a non-technical popular presentation of Vallabācārya's thought on the nature of the Supreme Reality, Man and the Wolrd and *not* a critique of his philosophy. I may, however, notice two Śaiva teachers.

Śrīkaṇṭha (circa AD 1300)

Śrīkaṇṭha is a Śaiva *viśiṣṭādvaitin*. He was probably a contemporary of Rāmānuja, though his commentator Appaya Dīkṣit suggests that Rāmānuja follows Śrīkaṇṭha. He calls his commentary on the *BrSū* as *Brahma-Mīmāṁsā Bhāṣya* or *Aupaniṣadī Mīmāṁsā*, though he has freely used Āgamas as authoritative texts along with Śruti. Though mainly a supporter of Viśiṣṭādvaita doctrine, he tilts to Advaita in interpreting some *sūtras* (see G.V. Tagare — *Śaiva Darśana*, pp. 162-64) and particularly to Kāśmīr Śaivism.

God does not transform himself into the world but it is His Śakti which manifests herself as the world. He is both Knowledge and Knower. His *cit śakti* consists of knowledge (*jñāna*), volition (*icchā*) and action (*kriyā*). His *acit-śakti* consists of elements like earth, water, etc., the *cit* and *acit*, — Non-difference between the *Brahman* and *Prapañca* means mutual interdependence and not identity. The Universe is *Brahma-pariṇāma*, i.e. transfiguration of His *cit-śakti*.

The soul is an eternal and real substance, doer, an enjoyer, an active agent, atomic in size. God only helps the realization of each one's wishes. He is neither cruel nor partial.

Meditation of the Lord in his own nature leads to liberation directly and immediately.

Mokṣa: The grace of the Lord is the essential prerequisite for *mokṣa*. The freed souls are omniscient, independent, similar to the Lord but not identical with Him, for the soul is atomic and the Lord is all-pervading. Liberation is after death. There is no *jīvan-mukti* according to Śrīkaṇṭa. The infulence of Kāśmīr Śaivism is strong on Śrīkaṇṭha.

Śrīpati Paṇḍit (AD 1500?)

Śrīpati Paṇḍit, an Āndhra brāhmaṇa from Vijayavāḍā wrote a commentary on the *BrSū* from difference-cum-non-difference (*dvaitādvaita*) point of view. As a Śaiva, he admitted the authority of twenty-eight Śaiva Āgamas but not of Tāntric texts like Rāmānuja. He accepts unity in duality on the analogy of a serpent and its coils. Para-Śiva or the *Brahman* is the primary cause of everything and as such the reality of the world (*BrSū*, II.22.28). This *sūtra* maintains the existence of external objects due to their perception. This repudiates the *māyā* doctrine which holds all objects illusory and non-existent. He explains that as Śiva is their *upādāna kāraṇa*, they are not *mithyā* (illusory)

(I.1.1). He repudiates Śaṅkara's theory of world appearances and formless *Brahman* as unworthy of acceptance (I.1.20).

The soul is beginningless, atom-like, bound down by *māyā* but has the freedom to act and realise Śiva.

Mokṣa

So long a soul is fettered by *māyā*, there is *Dvaita* (Duality or difference) between the soul and the *Brahman*, the freed soul is Śiva-like in form (*śiva-sārūpya*), omniscient but retains his individuality. *Jīva* and *Brahman* are different from each other but in the progressive six stages — *ṣaṭ-sthala* — *jīva* attains Brahmahood with the grace of God and *guru*. On the analogy of *bhramara-kīṭa-nyāya*, the individual soul attains the nature of Śiva by worship and meditation.

Śrīpati's work forms a solid foundation to the Vīra-Śaiva Sect.

We may sum up the names of the important pre-Vallabha teachers and their doctrines.

Author	Doctrine
1. Śaṅkara (*circa* AD 700)	*Kevalādvaita*
2. Bhāskara (AD 1000)	*Bhedābheda*
3. Rāmānuja (AD 1017-1127)	*Viśiṣṭādvaita*
4. Madhva (*c*.1238)	*Dvaita*
5. Śrīkaṇṭha (*c*.1300)	*Śaiva Viśistādvaita*
6. Śrīpati Paṇḍit (*c*.1500)	*Dvaitādvaita*

Notes

1. Hakujui quoted by Hajime Nakamura in *A History of Early Vedantic Philosophy*, p. 183.
2. अस्पर्श-योगो वै नाम सर्व-सत्त्व-सुखो हि सः।
   अविवादो, अनिरुद्धश्च देशिनस्तं नमाम्यहम्।।
   — गौडपाद, माण्डुक्य-कारिका

3. अद्वैतं केचिदिच्छन्ति, द्वैतमिच्छन्ति चापरे।
समं तत्त्वं न विन्दन्ति द्वैताद्वैत-विवर्जितम्।।

4. अनिरोधम् अनुत्पादम्, अनुच्छेदम्, अशाश्वतम्।
अनेकार्थम्, अनानार्थम्, अनागमम्, अनिर्गमम्।।
न सन्, नासन्, न सदसन्, न चापि उभयात्मिकम्।
चतुष्कोटि-विनिर्मुक्तं तत्त्वं माध्यमिका विदुः।।

5. जीवो ब्रह्मैव नापरः।

6. Adapted from *History of Indian Philosophy : Eastern and Western*, Vol. I, pp. 279 ff.

7. यथा माया यथा स्वप्नो गन्धर्व-नगरं यथा।
तथोत्पादास्तथास्थानं तथा भङ्गा उदाहृताः।।

— *माध्यमक कारिका*, 7.34

8. विच्छिन्नमूलं महायानिक-बौद्ध-गाथितं मायावादं व्यावर्णयन् ते लोकान् व्यामोहयन्ति।

— Bhāskara on *BrSū*, 1.4.25

9. तत् (= ब्रह्मन्) कारणात्मना कार्यात्मना च द्विरूपेण अवस्थितम्।

— Bhāskara — *BrSū*, 1.1.4

10. ब्रह्मसूत्रपदैश्चैव हेतुमद्भिः सुनिश्चितैः।

— *BG*, 13.4

11. S. Radhaksishnan, *Brahmasūtra*, Intro., p. 46.

12. *Bratma Sūtras — Śrī Bhāṣya* by Svāmī Vīreśvarananda and Svāmī Ādidevānanda (Advaita Ashram, Calcutta), pp. xxv-xxvi.

13. S. Radhakrishnan, *Brahma Sūtra*, Intro., p. 57.

14. *Ibid.*, p. 65 fn. 1 quotes from Madhva's *Mahābhārata-Tātparya-nirṇaya.*

त्रिविधा जीवसङ्घास्तु देव-मानुष-दानवाः।
तत्र देवा मुक्तियोग्या मानुषेषूत्तम-स्तथा।।
मध्यमा मानुषा एते सृतियोग्यास्तदैव हि।
अधमा निरयायैव दानवास्तु तमोलयाः।।

5

The Concept of the Deity

UPTIL now we have seen the main stages in the evolution of Indian thought with reference to the Deity, Man and the World. It was mainly with reference to the Upaniṣadic concepts to which we limited ourselves with occasional references to non-Vedic systems of thought. Our main object is to understand the elements of *Brahma-Vāda* as taught by the great Ācārya Vallabha.

The term *Brahma-Vāda* originally meant 'religious discussion' (with special reference to Vedic literature, specifically the Vedānta or the Upaniṣads). Later on it came to mean 'Discussion on the *Brahman*' (as the *Brahman* was the most important part of Upaniṣadic discussiouns). Śaṅkara uses it as a technical term to mean the philosophical position of his school. In his commentary, he calls his school *Aupaniṣada Darśana* (*BrSū*, 2.2.10) and his doctrine *Vedānta-Vāda* (*BrSū*, 1.4.22) but *never māyā-vāda*. It was his earliest critic, Bhāskara, exponent of 'difference-cum-non-difference' (*bhedābheda-vāda*) who, probably as an opponent, called Śaṅkara a *māyā-vādin* (*Com.* on *BrSū*, 2.1.14, 4.4.14). As H. Jacobi points out: the *māyā-vāda* concept recognises the reality of the *Brahman*, the rest is completely phantasmagoric and false (*JAOS*, 1913, p. 52). But as Paul Deussen points out: "Śaṅkara maintained the theory of the empirical reality of the external world" (*The System of the Vedānta*, p. 55, n.31, pp 241-44). Due to similarity betweeen some views in Śaṅkara's Vedānta and in the Mahāyāna Buddhism, Bhāskara, commenting upon *BrSū*, 2.2.29, calls *māyā-vādins* as 'dependent on Buddhism' (*Baudhha-matānuvādino māyāvādinaḥ*).

But to distinguish Vallabhācārya's Advaitic views from those of Śaṅkara, we designate his doctrine as *Śuddhādvaita*. The term means, 'Advaita uncontaminated by *māyā*.' As Ācārya Giridhara defines it:*

> It (the doctrine of *Śuddhādvaita*) is called Pure, unsoiled with any contact with *māyā*. The *Brahman* which is a cause as well as an effect in form (*kārya-kāraṇa-rūpa*) is pure and has no relation with *māyā*.
>
> *Śuddhādvaita Mārtaṇḍa*, VV 27-28

As stated in Vallabhācārya's biographical sketch, Vallabhācārya, the promulgator of the Śuddhādvaita school of philosophy, proclaimed himself as a follower of Viṣṇusvāmī of Kāñcī. It is said that Viṣṇusvāmī belonged to the Rudra School of Vaiṣṇavism and was a Dualist. He is credited to have written *bhāṣyas* on *Prasthāna Trayī*, but nothing except seven verses attributed to him have come down to us (*vide* Appendix II). But they do not constitute an adequate basis for the great edifice of Śuddhādvaita philosophy as expounded by Vallabhācārya.

Viṣṇusvāmī seems to be a historical person, as he is mentioned by Nābhādāsa (himself a southerner) in the *Bhaktmālā* (*chappayya* 48). The work was written in *Saṁvat* 1592 (*Hindi Śahitya Kośa*, part II, ed. by Dhirendra Varmā, *Saṁvat* 2020). Varmā records a hearsay information making Jñānadeva, Trilochana and Vallabha as followers of Viṣṇusvāmī.

The sacred *mantra* communicated by Viṣṇusvāmī for *japa* and meditation is *Gopāla Mantra*. The *mantras* of *puṣṭi-mārga*, promulgated by Vallabhācārya are:

(1) *Kṛṣṇa tavāsmi.*

Oh Kṛṣṇa, I am yours (You are my Master)

(2) *Śrīkṛṣṇaḥ śaraṇam mama.*

Kṛṣṇa is my resort or shelter.[1]

---

*मायासम्बन्धरहितं शुद्धमित्युच्यते बुधैः।

कार्य-कारण-रूपं हि शुद्धं ब्रह्म, न मायिकम्।।

— गिरिधर in शुद्धाद्वैतमार्तण्ड VV 27-28

Both Viṣṇusvāmī and Vallabhācārya were ardent devotees of Kṛṣṇa. Vallabhācārya, however, inherited it from his family tradition.

Pramāṇas (Valid means of Knowledge)

Philosophy is a search for true knowledge. True knowledge can be acquired through valid means of arriving at the truth in reality. They use the term *pramā* for 'true knowledge' and *pramāṇa* for 'valid means of getting true knowledge'. All schools of Indian Philosophy, Vedic and non-Vedic have adopted these terms.

The Buddhists regard *pramāṇas* as 'valid avenues of knowledge that are not at variance with the Real'. Dharmakīrti (*c.* AD 635) in his *Pramāṇa-Vārttika* regards *pramāṇas* as 'the recognition of the uncognised'. According to Nyāya-Vaiśeṣikas, *pramāṇa* is 'the unfailing source of true knowledge'.

Number of Pramāṇas

Different schools of Indian Philosophy have adopted different number of *pramāṇas* from one, viz., *pratyakṣa* (Perception) recognised by Cārvākas upto six *pramāṇas* accepted by the Bhaṭṭa school of Mīmāṁsakas. In between we have Vaiśeṣikas who recognise only two, viz., *pratyakṣa* (perception) and *anumāna* (Inference). Sāṁkhyas add the third *pramāṇa*, viz., *śabda* (Testimony). Naiyāyikas recognise four *pramāṇas*, viz., (1) *pratyakṣa* (Perception), (2) *anumāna* (Inference), (3) *upamāna* (Comprison or Analogy), (4) *śabda* (Testimony).

Prābhākara (Bhaṭṭa) Mīmāṁsakas add *arthāpatti* (Initial Doubt) as the fifth *pramāṇa*, while the other Mīmaṁsā school, viz., that of Kumārila Bhaṭṭa, adds (*anupalabadhi*) as the sixth *pramāṇa*. In *Arthāpatti* there must be an initial doubt which is to be resolved later *Anupalabdhi* is non-perception and it is recognised to explain the apprehension of *abhāva* (non-existence). Thus it is an instrument to know what does not exist.

Though the multiplicity of *pramāṇas* appears complex, we can reduce these six *pramāṇas* into three: (1) *pratyakṣa* should include *anupalabdhi* as it is only the absence of *pratyakṣa* (Perception), (2) *anumāna* accommodates *upamāna* and *arthāpatti* which are varieties of inference, (3) *śabda*.

By the way, I may point out that Mahāprabhu Caitanya, in his *Daśa-Mūla-Śloka* remarks that Logic has no competence in determining the *Ultimate Reality*. The Vedas (*śruti*), as the record of higher mystical experience of sages, are the true guide (to comprehend Reality).

Vallabhācārya's Views

Vallabhācārya recognises the following four *pramāṇas*: (1) *pratyakṣa* (perception), (2) *anumāna* (Inference), (3) *aitihya* (Tradition), (4) *śruti* — the corpus of Vedic literature including *Saṁhitās*, *Brāhmaṇas* *Āraṇyakas* and *Upaniṣads*.

Vallabhācārya specifically emphasizes Śruti (Vedas) as *THE* only *pramāṇa* as they constitute the supernatural, in matters of supernatural subjects, self-evident, self-proved (*svataḥ-siddha pramāṇa*)[1] (see *TDN*,1.7).

In Śrutis, *Saṁhitā, Brāhmaṇa* and *Āraṇayaka* comprise the ritualistic section (*karma-kāṇḍa*), while Upaniṣads (the older strata) constitute the philosophical section (*jñāna-kāṇḍa*). As these are *dharmas* (Attributes) of *Paramātman*, these two are in a way one and the same. These two *kāṇḍas* being complementary to each other are regarded as identical.[2] According to Vallabhācārya, the authoritative texts under *śabda* are the *Bhagavad Gītā* (*BG*) the *Brahma Sūtras* (*BrSū*) and the *Bhāgavata Purāṇa* (*BhP*) *in general*.[3]

In the case of *BhP*, Vallabhācārya regards that only the meditational part (*samādhi bhāṣā*) of Vyāsa, should be regarded as authoritative. While explaining what he means by *samādi bhāṣā*, Vallabhācārya excludes the following portion from the *BhP* as unauthoritative.

(1) Ordinary description or narrative, e.g.

atha uṣasi upavṛttāyām

When it dawned —*BhP*, X.70.1

(2) Quotations or what is heard from others:

śrutaṁ dvaipāyana-mukhāt

Heard from the mouth (i.e. oral speech) of Dvaipāyana

Thus by *samādhi bhāṣā* of Vyāsa, Vallabhācārya means what Vyāsa expressed after experiencing it while in a trance (*samādhi*)[4] or philosophical verses.

The words *caiva* added after *Vyāsa-Sūtrāṇi*, i.e. *Brahma Sūtra* in *TDN*, 1.7 imply the *Pūrva-Mīmāṁsā śāstra* of Jaimini. Vallabhācārya is credited to have written a commentary on those *sūtras*.

Traditionally, logic or reasoning was given a secondary place in search of spiritual reality. This (spiritual) knowledge cannot be obtained by Logic or reasoning (*tarka*),[5] declares the *Kaṭha Upaniṣad* (II.7). *BrSū* (2.1.11) regards *tarka* as of 'ill-foundation' (*a-pratiṣṭhāna*). In explaining the reason for *tarka* being declared 'unfounded', Rāmānuja says,. "Theories based on human reasoning are liable to be upset or modified by people more skilled in reasoning (as found in the disputation of other sects).[6] Vallabhācārya endorses the same view.[7]

Gradation of Pramāṇas

Out of *pramāṇas* recognised by Vallabhācārya, namely the Vedas, the *Bhagavad Gītā*, the *Brahma Sūtras* and the *Bhāgavata Purāṇa*, the consecutively latter *pramāṇa* removes doubts that have remained in spite of the previous *pramāṇa*.[8] Whatever does not conform to the consensus of these (even if it be the *Manusmṛti*) is not a *pramāṇa*[9] in the matter of the subjects dealt in the *Śāstrārtha Prakaraṇa* (of *TDN*) and not in the matter of *Varaṇāśramācāra-lakṣaṇa-dharma* (*Sarvanirṇaya Prakaraṇa* of *TDN*).

Prameya: The Brahman: Kṛṣṇa

The Ultimate Reality to be ascertained by the *pramāṇas* is the *Para Brahman* or Śrī Kṛṣṇa, as he devoutly designates it. Kṛṣṇa was the hereditary deity in his family. Kṛṣṇa is called the *Brahman* in the Vedānta. *Paramātmā* in Smṛtis and *Bhagavān* in the *BhP*.[10] The *Karma-Kāṇḍa*, describes Him as *yajña* (sacrifice); the *Jñāna-Kāṇḍa* (Vedānta) describes Him as the *Brahman*, endowed with the special powers of Knowledge, while the *Bhāgavta* describes Him as *Avatārin*[11] i.e. one who takes all incarnations. Vallabhācārya describes Kṛṣṇa as the supreme *Brahman* characterised by *sat* (existence), *cit* (consciousness) and *ānanda* (Bliss) vide *Siddhānta-muktāvali*.[12]

The Concept of the Brahman

Though the grammatical gender of the vocable *Brahman* is neuter, I use He to designate Him, as Vallabhācārya regarded Kṛṣṇa as another name for the *Brahman*.

As noted above, Kṛṣṇa or the *Brahman* is the Supreme Reality. He is one and only one without a second. He is Existence (*sat*), Consciousness (*cit*) and Bliss (*ānanda*). He is the material and instrumental cause in the creation of the World. By His sheer will, He creates and maintains the world and by His sheer will, He withdraws it in Him (*pralaya*). Here one is reminded of a similar concept about Parama Śiva and his *vimarśa* power. Vallabhācārya's concept about the *Brahman* may be better summarised by a quotation fron *BhP*, 10.8.54 wherein sage Śuka addresses Kṛṣṇa:

> You are the place (substratum), the agent and the instrument (i.e. the instrumental cause) of the Universe. You are the source of the Universe, its object or purpose, whenever and whatever form it assumes, is yourself. As and when this Universe evolves, all the causes thereof including time and manner, are the Almighty Lord yourself who controls both *prakṛti* (to be enjoyed, the object of enjoyment) and *puruṣa* (the enjoyer) and transcends them both.[13]
>
> (*BhP*, 10.85.4)

He is both the formless and endowed with a form.[14] He is both *saguṇa* (possessor of attributes) and *nirguṇa* (attributeless or devoid of undesirable qualities). He is a repository of contradictory qualities or attributes (*viruddha-guṇāśrayatva*). His powers and attributes are natural, that is, non-different from Him, as there is no difference or distinction between a quality or attribute (*dharma*) and the possessor of that *dharma* or attribute (i.e. *dharmin*). Here one is reminded of the fundamental doctrine of Kāśmīr Śaivas who regard that there is no difference between *śakti* (power) and the possesssor of power (*śaktimat*). They say:

śakti-śaktimator abhedaḥ

Thus *Brahman* Himself is Bliss, Consciousness and Existence *incarnate*.

The *Bhrahma-Vāda* emphasises the one-ness of *jaḍa*, *jīva* and *antaryāmin*. As contrasted with Rāmānujan, Vallabhācārya does not condemn *jaḍa* to remain so for ever. He says that in *jaḍa* (matter, material objects) there is only *sat* (the quality of Existence), in *jīva* (the animates) there are (the qualities) of *sat* (existence) and *cit* (consciousness) and in the *antaryāmin* there are *sat*, *cit* and *ānanda* (Bliss). If the quality of *cit* is infused or developed in *jaḍa*, he becomes animate and with the infusion or development of Bliss, they become *anatṛyāmin* or *ānandākāras*.

Here Śaṅkara differs. He holds that the *Brahman* is *nirguṇa* and *nirākāra* (attributeless and formless). The theory may have proposed to avoid contradiction in the qualities or fomrs of the *Brahman*. But Vallabhācārya's theory of accomodation of contradictory qualities or attributes (*paraspara-virudha-dharmāśrayatva*) in the *Brahman* reconciles the probable objection by accepting this special characteristic of the *Brahman*.

There is one fundamental difference in the *Brahman* concept of Śaṅkara and Vallabha. Śaṅkara believes that the *Brahman* by itself is inactive. It cannot create the world by itself alone. It is only in association with *avidyā* that the creation of the Universe takes place. In other words *avidyā* becomes the real creator and the recognition of *avidyā* as a creator contradicts the non-duality (*a-dvaita-tva*) of the *Brahman*. The recognition of *avidyā* as the creator of the world negates the reality of the world. Vallabhācāry,however, regards the *Brahman* as the material and instrumental cause of the Universe and as the *Brahman* is real, the world, Hiss creation is real. He modifies or transforms Himself in various things or forms. Hence, His non-duality.

Śaṅkara firmly states that the *Brahman* is the reality while the world is illusion.

brahma satyam, jagan mithyā
(The word *mithyā* is properly untranslatable)

Rāmānuja's concept of God's person consisting of *cit* (conscious) and *acit (non-Conscious)* parts, consigns *jaḍa* to eternal *jaḍatva*. Vallabhācārya, however, thinks that the infusion of *cit* and *ānanda* can lift *jaḍa* to the highest stage.

Madhvācārya is a Dualist or rather Pluralist. To him the *Brahman* is *prameya*, but there is difference between the *Brahman*, the souls (all different *inter se*) and the world. The *Brahman* is the instrumental cause while *prakṛti* is the material cause of the world. The *Brahman* is endowed with attributes (*sa-dharmaka*) and non-accommodative of contradictory attributes.

Vallabhācārya's doctrine of the special quality of accommodation of contradictory attributes enables him to reconcile contradictory statements in Śrutis such as 'the *Brahman* is minuter than the minutest and greater than the greatest'. (*Kaṭha Upaniṣad*, 1.2.20) 'He is devoid of hands and feet but He runs quickly. He sees without eyes and hears without ears'. (*Śvetāśvatara Upaniṣad* 3.19)

The creation of the world is due to His volition of Fundamental Will. He Willed: 'I am alone: Let me be many". And He manifested Himself as *jīva* and *jagat*, without undergoing any change in Himself, as in the case of gold and ornaments. It is called *a'-vikṛta-pariṇāma-vāda*. The creation is looked upon as His sport (*līlā*).

As to the relation between the Lord and the created world, Vallabhācārya says that both are non-different (*ananya*) as the effect (*kārya* — created world) is included in the cause (*kāraṇa* — the *Brahman*) and there is no *Mithyātva* (illusoriness). He quotes *Chāndogya Upaniṣad*, 6.1.4. (*vācārambhaṇam . . . mṛttikā ityeya satyam*).[15] This is called *satkārya-vada*.

Impartiality of God

If the Lord has created the world, He should be impartial to all. But we find some persons are miserable, while some others are happy. The facile explanation is that God dispenses weal and woe as per good and bad deeds of people. If so, God is not the Almighty. The Lord set all the *maryādās* (limitations) of what is good or evil and willed that souls should be so dealt with. But as per *BrSū*, 3.2.28, the soul may do whatever actions he likes, the Lord decides the result of those. It is especially so in the case of *bhaktas* (devotees) that their sins get already destroyed as per Lord's will.[16] Viṭṭhalanātha in *Vidvan-maṇḍala* (p. 164) says that God created the world as a sport and hence the variety (of some souls being happy and some others miserable). One is reminded here of Abhinavagupta who says that it is the sport of Lord Śiva to bind down souls and then to release them (*Tantrāloka*, 8.32).[17] One more explanation is that as souls, laws, *karmans* and their fruits are created by God and are all forms of the Lord, the charge of Lord's partiality and cruelty is baseless.[18]

Modern minds do not accept this explanation.

The Doctrine of Grace

The doctrine that Liberation from *saṁsāra* depends on the Grace of the Lord and not on human efforts, is held both by Vaiṣṇavas and Śaivas. *Anugraha* (conferring of Grace) is one of the functions of Śiva. Similarly in *TDN*.1.47, Vallabhācārya asserts that *mukti* (liberation from *saṁsāra*) is attained by one who is blessed with the Grace of the Lord and not to anybody (or anything) else.[19]

This doctrine is of Upanisadic antiquity.[20] It was used by teachers to promote the cult of *bhakti*. Vallabhācārya, however, distinguishes between liberated souls who have attained it by *maryādā bhakti* and those who attained it through *puṣṭi bhakti*. Lord Kṛṣṇa wishes to liberate followers of *puṣṭi bhakti* even though they have not acquired the requisite merit adequately. Vallabhācārya points out that owing to unfavourable (political, social etc.) circumstances, it is difficult to follow the paths of *karma* and *jñāna*. *Puṣṭi-mārga* is the pathway to God, The Upaniṣadic declaration is:

There is no other way (to go *mokṣa*).

The Doctrine of Avatāra

Vallabhācārya believes that as per *BG*, X — the chapter on *Vibhūti-Yoga* — especially vv 40-41 in which after enumerating celebrities in a number of different fields, Kṛṣṇa says, "There is no end to the persons endowed with my Supreme power (*vibhūti*) and if there is anyone endowed with Supreme power (*vibhūti*), he/she should be regarded as born of a portion (*aṁśa*) of my lustre."[21] Thus in addition to the ten usually believed as incarnations of Viṣṇu such as Divine Fish, Tortoise, and others, Vallabhācārya adds famous personalities from Pāñcarātra system and Vaiṣṇava Āgamas such as Manu, Ṛṣabha, Mahīdāsa, Vyāsa, Kapila and others.

As in the *BhP*, Vallabhācārya regards Kṛṣṇa as the perfectly complete incarnation of the *Para Brahman* and is endowed with both Knowledge (*jñāna*) and Action (*kriyā*) for which Kāśmīr Śaivas use the terms *prakāśa* and *vimarśa*. He Himself is the *Bhagavān*:

kṛṣṇas tu bhagavān svayam

The purpose of an *avatāra* is to remove the internal agony (of *saṁsāra*, the *antar-duḥkha*) and Vyāsa, Kapila or Dattātreya are thus representatives of *avatāras* of the *jñāna* power of the Lord. The other object of taking an *avatāra* is to remove the external miseries as is done by the Divine Fish, Tortoise, Man-Lion, etc.

There is a third category of *avatāras* called *āveśāvatāras* or *āvirbhāvas* — Persons inspired with divine power for a particular task. They are considered equal to other *avatāras* as there is no essential difference between the two (*viśeṣābhāvāt āveśāvatārāyoḥ tulayatayā gaṇanā*, *TDN*, III 1.49).

The *Para Brahman* will be attained through Devotion to the *ādhidaivika* aspect of the Reality.

Before I conclude I should state what the *BrSū* regards as *Brahman*'s identity with the following. This is a random sampling of the identification of the *Brahman* with:

Vaiśvānara (1.2.28), *Brahman* (1.3.8). *Akṣara* (1.3.10), *Dahara* (*Ākāśa* within 1.3.14), Universal Light (1.3.22), Divine Light, *Jyotiṣ* (1.3.40), *Ākāśa* (1.3.41). This randon sampling will show that the author of the *BrSū* has recognised the all-pervasiveness of the *Brahman*. Tomes have been written on the topic of the *Brahman*. In this chapter I have limited myself to give some important glimpses of Vallabhācārya's views regarding the *Brahman*.

Notes

1. शब्द एव प्रमाणम्। तत्राप्यलौकिक-ज्ञापकमेव।
ततः स्वतः सिद्ध-प्रमाण-मात्रं प्रमाणम्।
— *तत्त्वार्थ-दीप-निबन्ध* (*तदीनि*), I.7 comm.
2. काण्ड-द्वयस्य अन्योन्योपकारित्वाय साधारणग्रहणम्।
—*Aṇubhāṣya* (*AB*, I.1.2, p. 120)
also वेदाः सर्व एव काण्डद्वयस्थिता अर्थवादादिरूपा अपि।
— *तदीनि*, I. 6, comm., p. 35
3. वेदाः श्रीकृष्णवाक्यानि व्याससूत्राणि चैव हि।
समाधिभाषा व्यासस्य प्रमाणं तच्चतुष्टयम्।।
— *तदीनि*, I.7, pp. 36-37
4. यत्समाधौ अनुभूय निरूपितं सा सभाधिभाषा।
— *तदीनि*, I.7, p. 38
5. नैषा तर्केण मतिरापनीया।
— *कठ उपनिषद्*, 2.7
6. शाक्य-औलुक्य-अक्षपाद-क्षपणक-कपिल-पतञ्जलि-तर्काणामन्योन्यव्याघातात्।
Vallabhācārya quotes *BrSū*, 2.1.11 and remarks तर्को नाम स्वोत्प्रेक्षिता युक्तिः। सा एकोक्ता नान्यैरङ्गीक्रियते। स्वतन्त्राणा मृषीणां मतिभेदात् etc. (*Ibid.*, Vol. III, pp. 45-46).
7. *तदीनि*, शास्त्रार्थ प्रकरण, I. 62. Vallabhācārya. iterates अलौकिकं तत्प्रमेयं न युक्त्या प्रतिपद्यते।
8. उत्तरं पूर्वसन्देहवारकं परिकीर्तितम्।
— *तदीनि*, I. 8-A
9. अविरुद्धं तु यत्वस्य प्रमाणं तच्च नान्यथा।
— *तदीनि*, I. 8-A
10. वेदान्ते च स्मृतौ ब्रह्मलिङ्गं भगवते तथा।
ब्रह्मेति, परमात्मेति, भगवानिति शब्दयते।।
— *तदीनि*, I. 6
11. यज्ञरूपो हरिः पूर्वकाण्डे ब्रह्मतनुः परे।
अवतारी हरिः कृष्णः श्रीभागवत ईयते।।
— *तदीनि*, I.11
12. परं ब्रह्म तु कृष्णो हि सच्चिदानन्दकं बृहत्।
— *सिद्धान्त मुक्तावलि*, 3 A

13. यत्र, येन, यतो, यस्य, यस्मै यद् यद् यथा यदा।
स्यादिदं भगवान् साक्षात् प्रधान-पुरुषेश्वरः।।

— *श्रीमद्भागवत,* 10.85.4

14. उभयव्यपदेशात्त्वहिकुण्डलवत्।

— *BrSū*, 3.2.27

15. आरम्भणशब्दादिभ्यस्तदनन्यत्वं प्रतीयते। कार्यस्य कारणानन्यत्वं न मिथ्यात्वम्।

— AB on *BrSū*, II. 1.14

16. AB on *BrSū*, 3.3.28 छन्दत उभयाविरोधात्: तथा च भक्तिमार्गीयाणामपि पूर्व पापनाशो यः स भगवदिच्छाविरोधतः।

17. स्वयं बध्नानि देवेशः स्वयमेव विमुञ्चति।

— *तन्त्रालोक,* 8.82

18. आत्मसृष्टेर्न वैषभ्यं नैर्घृण्यं चापि विद्यते।

— *तदीनि,* I. 76

19. कृष्णप्रसादयुक्तस्य नान्यस्येति विनिश्चयः।

— *तदीनि,* I. 47

20. नायमात्मा प्रवचनेन लभ्यः, न मेधया, न बहुना श्रुतेन।
यत्रैवेष वृणुते तेन लभ्यः तस्यैष आत्मा विवृणुते तनुं स्वाम्।।

— *कठ उपनिषद,* 2.22, *मुण्डक उपनिषद,* 3.2.3

21. नान्तोऽस्ति मम् दिव्यानां विभूतीनाम्। — *BG*, X. 40
यद् यद् विभूतिमत्सत्त्वं श्रीमदूर्जितमेव वा . . . मम तेजोंऽशसम्भवम्।

— *BG*, X. 41

6

The Concept of Akṣara Brahman

WHAT is *akṣara Brahman*? It IS *Brahman* but a special aspect of it which was as if a forgotten chapter in Indian Philosophy.[1] Vallabhācārya deserves the credit of inviting attention to this aspect. Hence a special chapter is devoted to this topic.

Śaṅkara noted two grades of the *Brahman*.

(1) *Saguṇa* — Endowed with attributes, and

(2) *Nirguṇa* — Attributeless.

Vallabhācārya, in his usual way, hypothesized the following three grades or forms or aspects of the *Brahman*[2] as follows:

(1) *The ādhidaivika* — The *Para Brahman par excellence* or Kṛṣṇa or Puruṣottama.

(2) *The ādhyātmika* — The *Akṣara Brahman*. The *antaryāmin*, Principlc dwelling in finite souls.

(3) *The ādhibhautik* — The *Jagat*.

These are distinguished from each other by the 'Bliss' aspect. In *jagat* due to the Will of the Lord to be many, the bliss-aspect is eclipsed.

Epithets of the Akṣara Brahman[3]

(1) *Ādhāra* — Support of Puruṣottama

(2) *Caraṇa* — A foot of Puruṣottama

(3) *Avyakta* —The unmanifest

(4) *Vyoman or ākāśa* — The ether

(5) *Brahman* — As distinguished from *Para Brahman*

(6) *Mukhya jīva* — The life principle *par excellence*

(7) *Kūṭastha* — The immutable

(8) *Nirvikāra* — The unchanging

(9) *Parama dhāman* —The highest abode or the *summum bonum* of the *jñānins*. The highest abode to the devotees of the Lord.

(10) *Parama vyoman* — The Highest Ether

(11) *Haṁśa puccha* — The Tail of a Swan, viz,. the *ānanda-maya* Brahman

Concept of the Akṣara Brahman

The above list of epithets of the *akṣara Brahman*, throws light on various aspects of the concept of this *Brahman* as follows:[4]

Out of those forms of the *Brahman* mentioned above, Kṛṣṇa or Puruṣottama is the complete Supreme *Brahman* — the highest Bliss (*ānanda*) and sweetness (*rasa*). He is Bliss *par excellence*. He dwells in all, as the inner controller and is called *antaryāmin*.

Vallabhācārya explains *BrSū*, 1.2.21: "With slight obscuration of Bliss, the *Brahman* is called *akṣara*.[5] When due to the will of the Lord, His joy gets diminished in the capacity", it is called *Gaṇitānandakam* — as if it is a limited Bliss. Vallabhācārya indicates thereby that the *akṣara Brahman* is inferior to Kṛṣṇa or Puruṣottama whose Bliss is completely explicit.[6] (See *BrSū*, III.3.34)

In fact, it is the Supreme Soul who becomes both *puruṣa* and *prakṛti* at the beginning of the creation. It is that form of the Supreme that is called *akṣara*.[7]

The *akṣara Brahman* is distinct from the *para Brahman* and also from individual souls who emanate from Him like sparks from fire.

It is through the Will of the *para Brahman* that the *akṣara Brahman* assumes or appears to assume the following four forms.[8] (S. Radhakrishnan — *The Brahma Sūtra*, Intro., pp. 89-90)

(1) *Akṣara* itself which appears as *prakṛti* and *puruṣa* and is the cause of everything.

(2) *Kāla* (Time): It is regarded as a form of God. It is supra-sensible and is inferred from the nature of the effects (*kāryānumeya*). It is all-pervasive and is the cause that disturbs the equilibrium of *guṇas*.

(3) *Karma* or action is also universal. It manifests itself as different actions in different men.

(4) *Svabhāva* is that which produces change (*pariṇāma-hetutvam tallakṣaṇam*)

The above four forms are eternal principles, one with the Lord. The *akṣara* form manifests itself as *prakṛti* and *puruṣa* and becomes the cause of everything in the universe. When, at the time of creation, the Bliss of the *akṣara Brahman* becomes obscured, it is called *mukhya jīva*. It is superior to (other) *jīvas*. The Will of God when it materializes, becomes *prakṛti*. The *akṣara Brahman* is superior both to *prakrṛti* and *puruṣa* and contains within him millions of worlds along with their protective coverings (*āvaraṇas*). As *TDN,* II.96 state: *sarvāvaraṇa-yuktāni tasmin aṇḍāni koṭiśaḥ*.

As the spiritual form of *para Brahman*, the *akṣara Brahman* incarnated as *puruṣa* among other incarnations of the Lord.

As the spiritual form of *para Brahman*, the *akṣara Brahman* is the object of mediation of *jñāninis*. There by they finally merge with it. The four forms mentioned above are created from him. By the *upāsanā* (adoration and knowledge gained thereby) one becomes one with the Supreme *ātman*. Here Auḍulomi's view deserves notice. (*Vide* supra, p. 28).

Difference with other Vaiṣṇava Schools

It is not that Vallabhācārya differed only from Śaṅkara. He has serious philosophical differences with other Vaiṣṇava teachers also. Thus Rāmānuja's concept of *cit* and *acit* (i.e. *jaḍa* or non-conscious) being a part of the Lord's person is known as Viśiṣṭādvaita. He holds that the *jaḍa* or non-consious parts of God's person shall remain so eternally.

But Vallabhācārya holds that if even a portion (*aṁśa*) of consciousness (*cit*) and bliss (*ānanda*) were to manifest in *jaḍa* (*acit*) it becomes one with the *Brahman*, *cit* becoming identical with *Brahman* by the appearance of some glimpse of bliss (*ānanda*) Vallabhācārya does not condemn *jaḍa* eternally to the state of *jaḍatva* (non-consiousness). Rāmānuja does not accept that the *Brahman* is the receptable of contradictory attributes (*viruddha-dharmāśrayatva*) as stated by Vallabhācārya.

Vallabhācārya holds that there is no difference between the *Brahman, jīva* and *jagat*. But Madhva, a realist, regards that God, individual souls and the world are different *inter se*. He accepts perception (*pratyakṣa*), inference (*anumāna*) and *śabda* (Vedic authority) as the three *pramāṇa*s (valid means of knowledge). Madhva regards the *Brahman* as a possessor of attributes, but Vallabhācārya regards *Brahman* as endowed with both attributes (*sadharmaka*) and attributelessness (*nidharmaka*). In other words, Madhva does not accept that the *Brahman* is a receptacle of contradictory attributes. About causation Madhva regards *Brahman* as the Instrumental cause and *māyā* as the material cause (*upādāna*) of the world. Vallabhācārya does not accept *māyā* to have independent existence apart from *Brahman*, and regards *Brahman* as both the material and instrumental cause of the world. Madhva does not accept the concept of *akṣara Brahman* as enunciated by Vallabhācārya.

Rāmānuja and Madhva belonged to an earlier period. Hence we should regard that Vallabhācārya did not accept the above mentioned views as advocated by them.

Notes

1. G.H. Bhatt, *History. of Indian Philosophy, Eastern and Western*, Vol. I, p. 350.
2. सर्वेषां त्रिगुणत्त्वाद् हि त्रयो भेदाः पृथड्.मताः।
   आधिभौतिकमध्यात्ममधिभूतमिति स्मृताः।।
   — तदीनि, II. 119.
3. B.M. Dhruva, *An Introduction to the Śuddhādvaita School of Philosophy*, pp. 53-54.

4. *The concept of akṣara Brahman:*
प्रकृतिः पुरुषश्चोभौ परमात्माऽभवत् पुरा।
यद् रूपं समधिष्ठाय तदक्षरमुदीर्यते।।
आनन्दांश-तिरोभावः सत्त्वमात्रेण तत्र हि।
मुख्यजीवस्ततः प्रोक्तः सृष्टीच्छावशगो हरिः।
इच्छामात्रात् तिरोभावः तस्यायमुपचर्यते।
ब्रह्म-कूटस्थव्यक्तादि-शब्दैर्वाच्यो निरन्तरम्।।
सर्वावरणयुक्तानि तस्मिन् पिण्डानि कोटिशः ।
मूला विच्छेदरूपेण तदाधारतया स्थितः।
प्रभुत्वेन हरेः स्फूर्तौ लोकत्वेन तदुद्भवः।
अन्तर्याम्यत तारादि – रूपे पादत्वमस्य हि।।
हंसाकृतित्व-कथने पुच्छत्वं परमात्मनः।
तदुपासनया ज्ञानात् परमात्मात्वमस्य हि।।

— *तदीनि*, II. 99-103

5. पुरुषस्य ब्रह्मत्वं निःसंदिग्धमेव। ईषदानन्द-तिरो-भावेन ब्रह्माक्षरमुच्यते। प्रकटानन्दः पुरुष इति . . . . तस्माद दृश्यत्वादिगुणकः परमात्वैव।

— AB on *BrSū*, I.2.21 (Vol. II, p. 563)

6. On इयदामननात् (*BrSū*, 3.3.34) Vallabhācārya explains: इयदिति परिमाण वचनम् Quoting *तैत्तिरीय उपनिषद*, 2.8-A indicate multiple grades of joy of men, of Gandharvas, etc., and finally the bliss of the *Brahman* i.e. *akṣara Brahman* is regarded hundred fold that of Prajāpati. Thus *iyat* means 'measurable' up to a particular limit to quote Vallabhācārya: इयत् एतावदित्यक्षरानन्दस्य सावधिकत्वेन श्रुतौ कथनानंदमयत्वेन निरवध्यानन्दात्मकत्वस्य पुरुषोत्तमे कथनात्तथोक्ति।

— AB. on 3.3.34 (Vol. IV, p. 329)

7. प्रकृतिः पुरुषश्चोभौ, etc., is quoted above as तदीनि, II. 99; *BG* says
यस्मात्क्षरमतीतोऽहमक्षरत्दपि चोत्तमः।
अतोऽस्मि लोके वेदेऽस्मिन् प्रथित्तः पुरुषोत्त्मः।।

— *BG*, 15.18

8. S. Radhakrishnan, *The Brahma Sūtra*, Intro., pp. 89-90.

7

The Individual Soul (Jīvātman)

VARIOUS speculations about *jīvātmān* or individual soul — right from the denial of its very existence up to its identification with the Supreme *Brahman* — have been expressed by Indian Philosophers. Thus Canonical Buddhism denies the necessity of the hypothesiss called 'individual Soul'. (The *nairātmya* theory). The Prābhākara school of Mīmāṁsā regards the soul or Self as unconscious or *jaḍa* even in the state of liberation. The other great Mīmāṁsā teacher, Kumārila Bhaṭṭa holds that the Self or soul is conscious; that it has *jñāna-śakti*, even during sleep and an eternal unity of subject and object (a tilt towards the Vedānta). The Naiyāyikas regard the Self an eternal, indestructible and an infinite substance beyond space and time. It has consciousness as an adventitions quality (*āgantuka caitanya*).

Vallabha's Concept of the Soul

For the presentation of the views of Vallabhācārya on the individual Soul (*jīva*), it will be convenient to state the interpretations of Vallabhācārya, from the beginning of the topic on the soul in the *BrSū*, viz., from *BrSū*, II.3.16.

On the strength of Śrutis (Upaniṣads) like *Kaṭha*[1] and *Bṛhadāraṇyaka*,[2] Vallabhācārya asserts the eternity of *jīvas*. They are not created but they emerge out of the *Brahman* like sparks from fire. As he states in *TDN* (*Tattvārthaa-Dīpa-Nibhanda*)[3], it was due to the Will of the Lord that all formless souls were created like sparks from fire. But this emanation (from fire) of sparks is not creation.[4]

The souls are associated with the body in a secondary (*bhākta*) sense. The presence of *jīva* is felt when he is connected with the body and not when he is dissociated with it. When Devadatta is born, it is the body that is born and not that the *jīva* is created. When *jātakarma* and other *saṁskāras* of Devadatta are performed, they are applied to the body of Devadatta and not to the Soul. It is only in a secondary sense (*bhākta*) that they are attributed to the Soul. Thus birth and death refer to the body only and figuratively to the souls connected with the body.[5] *BrSū* (2.3.17) asserts the eternity of the Soul:[6] "The soul . . . being eternal (as it is known) from Śruti Texts."

The Attributes of the Soul

The first attributes of the Soul is consciousness. Vallabhācārya interprets *jña* in *BrSū*, 2.3.18 as *caitanya-svarūpa*. He points out that the 'Knowledge' of the soul is accepted by Śrutis. Rāmānuja and Nimbārka interpreted *jña* as both knowledge and knower. Vallabhācārya calls Śaṅkara "another incarnation of Mahāyānī Bauddha due to non-recognition of the distinction of *para Brahman* from *śarīrātmam*".[7] Besides this, Vallabhācārya's stand about the soul is: When it emanates from *akṣara (Brahman)*, it was both knower-cum-knowledge, but after obscuration of the Bliss-aspect, it remains merely consciousness, neither knowledge not the knower. But due to the artificial instruments, viz., mind (*manas*), intelligence (*buddhi*) and ego (*ahaṁkāra*) it becomes again knower as well as knowledge.

I think, from intuitional point of view, in spiritual experience, the soul transcends both as well as the relation between them. It is immaterial whether the soul is the knower or the knowledge.

The Size of the Soul (BrSū, 2.3.19-32)

The souls are atomic in size. They are innumerable but have the *Brahman* as their *antaryāmin* (indweller).

Vallabhācārya adduces the following grounds to prove the atomicity of the soul (as explained by Vallabhācārya)

1. Scriptures like the *Kauṣītakī Upaniṣad* (III.3) speak of the movements of the soul such as going out and returning (*utkrānti-*

gati-āgati). Such movement is impossible if the soul be all-pervasive (as held by Śaṅkara) or of body-size (as posited by Jains). Later on *BrSū*, 3.2.22, he quotes *Śvetāśvatara Upaniṣad* (V.9) to express the atomicity.[8] The word *sva* — in the next *sūtra, svātmanā* shows that the movements mentioned are strictly connected with the soul.[9]

2. The objection: How can an atomic soul occupying a part of the body feel sensation all over the body?

   Vallabhācārya (that is *BrSū*) replies: "Just as sandal-paste applied to one part of the body has a cooling effect all over the body (*BrSū*, 3.2.23) similarly the soul which occupies one part of body, viz., the heart[10] (*BrSū*, 3.2.24) experiences the pleasure and the pain extending all over the body.

3. The soul may be atomic in size but its inherent consciousness (viz., *caitanya guṇa*) is pervasive. Just as the fragrance of a rose or a *campaka* flower spreads out of the flower in the surrounding area, this atrribute (*caitanya guṇa*) of the Soul which resides in the heart, pervades all over the body to the tip of the finger and end of hairs. (*BrSū*, 2.3.23-27)

4. Śruti passages like *prajñayā śasrīraṁ samāruhya* (*Kauṣītakī Upaniṣad*, 3.6) show that intelligence is the *kāraṇa* and as such an attribute of the soul which is of atomic size. Śaṅkara regards *sūtras* up to this (*BrSū*, 23.19-28) as *pūrva-pakṣa*. But with due reference to Śaṅkara, I find *BrSū* seldom uses such a number of *sūtras* for *pūrva-pakṣa*.

5. It is generally believed that the great sentence (*mahāvākya*) *tat-tvam-asi* advocates the identity of the *Brahman* and the *ātman*. The *mahāvākya* is a part of *Chāndogya Upaniṣad* (6.9.4) which reads:

   sa ya eṣo'ṇimaitadātmyamidaṁ sarvaṁ
   tat satyam sa ātmā tat tvam asi śvetaka to

   Here *sa* (*ātmā*) is masculine and it cannot grammatically connected with *tat* (in the *mahāvākya*) which is grammatically the neuter gender. *Tat* must be connected with *aitadātmyam*.

The sentence thus should be

aitadātmyaṁ (Neut.gender) tat tvam asi

Aitadātmya means *brahmātmakatva* and not 'identify with the *Brahman*'. Thus according to Śruti quoted above, there is *no* identity *in toto* in the individual soul and the *Brahman*. Vallabhācārya points out that the identity is limited to *guṇa*s only. The most distinguishing *guṇa* of the *Brahman* is Bliss (*ānanda*). This is inherent in the *jīva*. It is however, latent in the *jīva* just as kingship is latent in the crown prince, (*rāja-jyeṣṭha-putra-vat*).[11] When the soul acquires that Bliss of *Brahman*, he becomes 'Brahmā-like'. But this position,viz., *brahmatā* is not *absolute* identity with the *Brahman*. When the soul is enmeshed in *saṁsāra*, the soul may not have the *ānanda* manifest in him but its potentiality is obscured — the inherent possession of *ānanda* in the soul cannot be denied.

This *ānanda* is just like virility (*puṁstva*) which exists in childhood but it becomes manifest after the attainment of youth.[12]

Vallabhācārya concludes that topic by stating that though Blissfulness (*ānanda*) is not manifest in the soul involved in *saṁsāra*, it is inherent in him though obscured and unmanifest. Texts like *tat-tvam-asi* imply similarity in the *guṇa*s of the individual soul and the *Brahman* and not complete identity between the two.

About the thumb-like size of the soul, Vallabhācārya believes it to be atom-like in size and its location is in the heart.

The Soul as an Agent (Kartā) (BrSū, 1.3.40)

Vallabhācārya refutes the view of Sāṁkhyas who attributes *kartṛtva* of an action, to *prakṛti*. Vallabhācārya states that it is to *jīva*s that Vedic passages, i.e. injunctions of prescription of *karma*s are laid down for obtaining felicity here and *mokṣa* hereafter. *Prakṛti*, being *jaḍa* is incapable of doing these (*jaḍasya aśakyatvāt*).[13]

Śruti mentions *jīva*'s freedom (and ability) to move in celestial world (*gandharva-lokeṣu*).[14] Sense-organs are mere instruments.[15] In the *Taittirīya Upaniṣad* (2.5.1), the term *vijñāna* in

vijñānam yajñam tanute karmāṇi tanute'pi ca[16]

is used in the sense of *jīva*, the possessor of *vijñāna* and performance of sacrifices are prescribed for *jīvas*. The Sāṁkhya interpretation attributes agency (*kartṛtva*) to *buddhi* and enjoyment to *jīva*. But *buddhi* being *jaḍa* is incapable of action. I may add: In *Bṛhadāraṇyaka Upaniṣad* (2.1.17) intelligence is said to be an instrument through which the soul acts. *Jīva* has both *kartṛtva* (agency) as well as *bhoktṛtva* (enjoyment of fruits of *karmans*). He is like a carpenter who makes a chariot (Agency) and enjoys a ride in it.[17] *Jīvas* are agents for themselves as well as for others.

It may be noted that the Soul is an agent when connected with adjuncts, i.e. sense-organs and *buddhi* (*BrSū*, 2.3.40).

Jīva's Dependence on the Brahman

The ability to act (*kartṛtva*) of the *jīva* is not absolutely independent. It depends on the *Brahman* of which it is a part. It may be argued that it is due to the contact with the *buddhi* that a *Soul* becomes an agent (*kartā*). But as *buddhi* is *jaḍa* (without consciousness) its contact cannot activate the *jīva*. Nor does the activity becomes manifest in the Soul due to his non-possession of Sense-organs. The view which condemns everything as illusory is not acceptable, as it is the view of Mādhyamika Bauddhas.

The *jīva* has inherited excellences like *aiśvarya*, etc., from the *Brahman*. The Śruti states that, "The Lord turns a *jīva* as (morally) bad if he wishes to degrade him and will get holy actions performed through him, if He wants to elevate him."[18] (*Kauṣītakī Upaniṣad*, 3.8) But this exposes the *Brahman* to the charge of partiality (*vaiṣamya*) and cruelty (*nairghṛṇya*).

But this is not the case. In granting fruits of *karmas*, he is the occasional cause in alotting equal fruits according to *karmas* to *jīvas* (*karmāpekṣa*). In commenting on *BrSū*, 2.3.42, Vallabhācārya writes in *sūtra*-Style.[19] For example: In granting of fruits, dependent on *karmas*, etc. (see Notes).

The Relation between the Individual Soul and the Brahman

In *Śāstrārtha Prakaraṇa* (27-30), Vallabhācārya lucidly states his views as follows:[20]

> In the beginning of creation, He (the *Brahman*) who was alone, desired to be many. Due to the Will of the *Brahman* and dependent on it, at first non-conscious objects with *sadaṁśa* (*sat,* i.e. merely existence as a part), and conscious beings (characterised by part-consciousness and intelligence) emanated from the *Brahman* like sparks from five. They are bereft of Bliss (*ānanda*) and are *nirīndriya* (devoid of Sense-Organs).

Here the gradation is worth noting:

> The *Brahman* has *sat* (Existence), *cit* (Consciousness) and *ānanda* (Bliss). Animate or intelligent beings have *sat* (existence) and *cit* (Consciousness) as the qualities and the Bliss part is obscured. When a *jīva*, through the dint of spiritual knowledge or *bhakti* regains his part of Bliss (*ānandāṁśa*), he ceases to be atomic and becomes *Brahma-like* and ubiquitous (*BrSū* devotees a long section. 2.3.42-53) to delineate the relations between the *jīva* and the *Brahman.* In the previous section the *Brahman* is said to be the controller of the *jīvas*. Now, the relation between them is like that of a master and servant or sparks and fire? Vallabhācārya holds that the *jīva* is an *aṁśa* (part) of the *Brahman* —
>
> *brahmā-vāde aṁśa-pakṣaḥ*

This position is confirmed in the *BG*, 15.7. The Lord says: A fragment of mine has become a living Soul and is eternal.[21] But the original, inherent Bliss-part (*ānandāṁśa*) of the soul is obscurred. Now if the *jīva* is a part of the *Brahman*, the latter must be affected by the misery, etc., of the *jīva*, just as some pain to the hand causes pain to the whole body. But while commenting on *BrSū*, 2.3.46 *prakāśādivan naiva paraḥ*. Vallabhācārya explains that (being affected) is not the case.

Prin. J.G. shah explains:

> The *sūtrakāra* allows the legality of the objection, but to strengthen his position he cites an analogous case of *prakāśa* (Light). We know that heat or light causes burning sensation in others, but heat itself is immune from it.

On '*nāgner hi tāpo, na himasya tat syāt*'. Vallabhācārya says "Fire is not scorched by the heat of the fire, nor the cold by its coldness."

J.G. Shah proceeds:

> Just as a *doṣa* (defect) of a lighted object does not affect the *prakāśa* (light), the defect (*doṣa*) of the *jīva*, a portion of *Brahman* does not affect it anyway.
>
> —*An Introduction to the Aṇubhāṣya* pp. 176-77.

Vallabhācārya quotes here a verse conveying the purport of the above argument:

> Just as the sun, the eye of all the worlds is not affected by external defects (troubles) of the eye, the Lord, the soul of all the people is not affected by the miseries of the people
>
> — *Kaṭha Upaniṣad,* 2.2.11 on *BrSū*, 2.3.43-46.

Vallabhācārya supports his argument by quoting from the *Śvetāśvatara Upaniṣad* in which we are told that out of the two birds perching on the same branch of a tree, one eats of the fruit of the tree while the other looks on without eating.[22] And also the *Kaṭha Upaniṣad* which declares that the *Brahman* is not affected by the eternal miseries of man.

Moreover, prescription of an act (*vidhi*) and prohibition (*niṣedha*) are prescribed for a *jīva* due to his connection with a particular body, mind, etc., and not to the incorporeal *Brahman*. Since individuals are different, there is no confusion in the miseries of a particular person with that of another (*BrSū*, 2.3.48-49).

Due to obscuratioon of *ānanda* (Bliss) the *jīva* is like a mere reflection of the sun seen in the water below (*BrSū*, 2.3.50).[23] But this reflection (*ā-bhāsa*) does not imply *mithyātva* of the *jīva* or the *Brahman*. The prescription and prohibition of duties (*anujñā-parihārau*) to a *jīva* are due to the relation (connection) of the *jīva* with a particular body. This does not create any difficulty in accepting the theory of *jīva*'s being a part of the *Brahman*.

Finally, Vallabhācārya rejects the theory of *adṛṣṭa*, an unseen principle of the nature of religious merits and demerits. Sāṁkhyas, Naiyāyikas also believe in the multiplicity of Souls. They explain the difference in the experiences of the pleasure and pain (*the bhoga-vyavasthā*) of the *jīvas* to their *adṛṣṭa*. The *BrSū*, rejects the hypothesis of *adṛṣṭa* (*BrSū*, 2.3.52) and even if it is accepted for the sake of argument, it is ineffective to mould the nature and the form of the *jīva*.

To sum up: According to Vallabhācārya:

I. Souls: Eternal, Uncreated

Individual souls are eternal and are not created by the *Brahman*.

II. Attributes of the Soul(s)

(1) Consciousness or possession of knowledge (*caitanya-svarūpa*).

(2) Size of the soul is atomic, spatially.

(3) Location — the heart, but pervades the whole body by its *caitanya-guṇa*.

(4) The Śruti text (*Chāndogya Upaniṣad* 6.9.4) states the similarity (*aitadātmya*) or likeness between the *Brahman* and the soul and not the identity *in toto*.

(5) Like the *Brahman*, the *jīva* has Bliss (*ānanda*) as an inherent *dharma* (quality) but it is latent or unmanifest while the *jīva* is enmeshed in *saṁsāra*.

(6) The *jīva* is both an agent (*kartā*) and enjoyer (*bhoktā*) of his *karmas*.

(7) The Agency (*kartṛtva*) of the Soul is not absolute but depends on the *Brahman*. But this does not imply partiality (*vaiṣamya*) and cruelty (*nairghṛṇya*) on the part of the *Brahman*. God dispenses fruits good or bad according to the past actions of the individual.

(8) Misery etc., of the *jīva* is due to *jīva*'s connection with the body.

(9) Individual souls are distinct and different. There is no confusion in their experience of *karma*.

III. Relations between the Jīva and the Brahman

The *jīva* is an *aṁśa* (part) of the *Brahman*. But the *Brahman* is not affected by the pleasure or pain of the *jīva*.

The distinct features of the *Brahman*, *jīva* and *jagat* (*jaḍa*) are as follows:

(1) *The Brahman*: Perfect Bliss (*ānanda*), *sat* (Existence) and *cit* (Consciousness).

(2) *The individual souls*: *Sat* (Existence), *cit* (Consciousness), but *ānanda* (Bliss) — dormant or latent.

(3) *The Jagat —the world*: *Sat* (Existence) only, *cit* (Consciousness) and *ānanda* (Bliss) are obscured.

(4) The *jīva* can regain Brahma-like Bliss through *bhakti* (Devotion) and realization of *Brahman*'s identity and can become Brahma-like and all-pervading.

(5) *Jīvas* are like reflections of the sun in water. Hence, the *Brahman* is not *affected* by the *karmans* of *jīvas*. But the analogy of reflection in water does not imply *mithyātva* of the *jīvas*.

(6) Like the two Upaniṣadic birds perching on the same branch of tree, the *Brahman* is merely an on-looker.

(7) The religious prescriptions (*vidhi*) and prohibitions (*niṣedha*) pertain to the body of the *jīva*.

(8) Vallabhācārya rejects the theory of *adṛṣṭa*. It is ineffective to mould the nature and form of *jīvas*.

Notes

1. न जायते म्रियते वा विपश्चिन्नायं कुतश्चिन्न बभूव कश्चित्।
अजो नित्यः शाश्वतोऽयं पुराणो न हन्यते हन्यमाने शरीरे।।
— कठ उपनिषद, 1.2.48

2. स वा एष महानज आत्माऽजरोऽमरोऽमृतोऽभयो।
ब्रह्माभयं वै ब्रह्माभयः वै ब्रह्म भवति य एवं वेद।।

— *बृहदारण्यक उपनिषद,* 4.4.25

3. सृष्टयादौ निर्गताः सर्वे निराकारास्तदिच्छया।
विस्फुलिंगा इवाग्नेस्तु सदंशेन जडा अपि।।

— *तदीनि,* I.28

4. विस्फुलिङ्गवदुच्चरणं नोत्पत्तिः। नामरूप संबंधाभावात्।

— AB on *BrSū*, 2.3.16 (Vol. III, p. 274)

5 शरीरस्यान्वय-व्यतिरेकाभ्यामेव जीवस्य तद्भावित्वम्।
देहधर्मो जीवस्य भाक्तः। तसम्बन्धेनैवोत्पत्ति-व्यपदेशः।।

— AB on *BrSū*, 2.3.16 (Vol.II, p. 270)

6. नाभृाश्रुते-र्नित्यत्वाच्च ताभ्यः।

— *BrSū*, 2.3.17

7. यः सर्वज्ञः सर्वशक्तिः। अयमात्मा अपहतपाप्मा। अधिकं तु भेदनिर्देशादित्यादिबाधः। तस्मात् तदंशस्य तद् व्यपदेशवाक्य-मात्रं स्वीकृत्य शिष्टपरिग्रहार्थं माध्यमिकस्यैवायमपरावतारः।

— AB on *BrSū*, 2.3.18 (Vol. III, p. 282)

8. बालाग्रशतभगस्य शतधा कल्पितस्य च।
भागो जीवः स विज्ञेयः।

—*श्वेताश्वतर उपनिषद,* 5-9

9. स्वात्मना जीवरूपेण गत्यागत्योः सम्बन्धी जीवः।
अतो मध्यमपरिमाणमयुक्तमिति अणुरेव भवति।।

— AB on *BrSū*, 2.3.20 (Vol. III, p. 290)

10. *हृदि हि* – हृदि जीवस्य स्थितिः।

— AB on *BrSū*, 3.2.24 (Vol. II, p, 290)

11. यावद् आत्मा ब्रह्म भवति आनन्दांशप्राकट्येन तावदेव तद्व्यपदेशो राजज्येष्ठपुत्रवत्।

— AB on *BrSū*, 2.3.30 (Vol. III, p, 325)

12. व्यपदेश-दशायामपि आनन्दांशस्य नात्यन्तमसत्त्वम्। यथा पुंस्त्वसेकादि सामर्थ्यं बाल्ये विद्यमानमेव यौवने प्रकाश्यते तथा आनन्दांशस्य अपि सत एव व्यक्तियोगः।

— AB on *BrSū*, 2.3.31 (Vol. III, p, 328)

Vallabhācārya supplements some verses from *TDN* (तदीनि), I. 53-54

व्यापकत्व-श्रुतिस्तस्य भगवत्वे न युज्यते ।। 53 ।।
आनन्दांशाभिव्यक्तौ तु तत्र ब्रह्माण्ड-कोटयः।
प्रतीयेरन् परिच्छेदो व्यापकत्वं च तस्य तत्।। 54।।

13. जीवमेवाधिकृत्य वेदेऽभ्युदय-निःश्रेयस्-फलार्थं सर्वाणि कर्माणि विहितानि . . . . जडस्य; अशक्यतवात्।

— AB on *BrSū*, 2.3.33 (Vol. III, p, 333)

14. *BrSū*, 2.3.34 and AB on it.
15. *BrSū*, 2.3.35 and AB on it.
16. *BrSū*, 2.3.36 and AB on it.
17. *BrSū*, 2.3.40 and AB on it.
18. एष ह्येव साधु कर्म कारयति तं यमेभ्यो लोकेभ्यः उन्निनीषते
एष उ एवमेनमसाधु। कर्म कारयति तं यमयो निनीषते।।

— कौषीतकी उपनिषद, 3.8

19. फलादाने कर्मापेक्षः कर्म-कारणो प्रयत्नापेक्षः। प्रयत्ने कामापेक्षः कामे मर्यादापेक्षः, इति मर्यादा-रक्षणार्थं वेदं चकार। ततो न ब्रह्मणि दोषगन्धोऽपि। न चानीश्वरत्वम्।

— AB on *BrSū*, 2.3.42 (Vol. III, pp, 357)

20. विस्फुलिङ्गा इवाग्रेर्हिजडजीवा विनिर्गताः।
सर्वतः पाणिपादान्तान् सर्वतोऽक्षिशिरोमुखान्।
निरीन्द्रियान् स्वरूपेण तादृशादिति निश्चयः।
सदंशेन जडाः पूर्वं चिदंशेनेतरे अपि।
अन्यधर्म तिरोभावान् मूलेच्छातोऽस्वतंत्रिणः।।

— *तदीनि, शास्त्रार्थ*, I.27-36

21. ममैवांशो जीवलोके जीवभूतः सनातनः।

— *BG*, 15-7

22. द्वा सुपर्णा सयुजा सखायः - - -
तयोरन्यः पिप्पठं स्वादु अत्ति।
अनश्नन् अन्यः अभिचाकशीति।।

— *श्वेतावश्वतर उपनिषद*, 4.6, *मुण्डक उपनिषद*, 3.1.1

23. सूर्यो यथा सर्वलोकस्य चक्षुः।
न लिप्यते चाक्षुषैर्बाह्यदोषैः।।
एकस्तथा सर्वभूतान्तरात्मा।
न लिप्यते लोकदुःखेन बाह्यः।।

8

The Jagat (World)

UPANIṢADS like the *Aitareya*[1] (1.1.1) state that being tired of loneliness, the Lord became many and what is, is the *Brahman* (*Chāndogya Upaniṣad,*[2] 3.14.1). This is the doctrine of the reality of the world (*jagat-satyatva*). *Jagat* emanated from the *Brahman*, like sparks from fire and is endowed with the characteristic called *sat* (existence).[3] The *jagat* is different from *saṁsāra* which is characterised by Transiency.

The *jagat*, which emanated from the *Brahman*, is a matter of perception. In commenting on *BrSū*, 2.2.28, Vallabhācārya refutes the doctrine of the *vijñānavādins* who hold that *prapañca* is beyond cognisance and hence non-existent. Vallabhācārya states that *prapañca* is actually cognised or seen. Hence it is a reality. He derides the comment by asking, "How can one believe in a man who denies what he see?"[4] In commenting on the next Sūtra:

vaidharmyācca na svapnādivat (BrSū, 2.2.29)

Vallabhācārya says:

> And on account of difference in nature (ideas of the waking state) are not like those in dream. The *sūtrakāra* means that these are ideas of two different natures. Those in dreams, illusions, etc., are different from those of the waking state. The ideas of dreaming state are negated in waking life, while those in waking state continue to exist without change.

As Vallabhācārya puts it:

> 'A pillar will remain a pillar even after many years.' Evan Śaṅkara admits that things apprehended in the waking state

> are not negated in any other state. He has also taken the example of a pillar.[5]

On the next *sūtra*, Vallabhācārya refutes the position of *vijñāna-vāda* as follows:

> *Vijñāna-vāda* attempts to account for the variety of ideas by the variety of mental impressions, without any reference to external objects. But without the perception of external objects, the existence of mental impressions is impossible. If it is argued that desires are beginningless, the statement will have the fault of 'Blind following the blind' (*andha-paramparā nyāya*). The positive and the negative methods of argument (*anvaya* and *vyatireka*) are in favour of the reality of objects.[6]

Rāmānuja argues that,

> We nowhere perceive conginitions not inherent a cognising subject and not referring to objects.

In *Brahma-Vāda*, the *Brahman* is regarded as *abhinna-nimittopādāna-kāraṇa* of the *jagat* and was stated in *BrSū*, 2.1.14, there is no material difference between cause and effect. If the caúse (the *Brahman*) is real, its effect (the *jagat*) is real. The *jagat* is the play of Kṛṣṇa wherein he assumes name and form.[7]

The Brahman: The Material Cause of Jagat

BrSū, 1.4.23 to 1.4.27 prove that the *Brahman* is the Material and the Efficient cause of the world. Their text may be briefly summarised here:

> (The *Brahman* is) the material cause also, for this view does not conflict with the initial statement and illustrations (1.4.23). It is so on account of action referring to itself owing to transformation (1.4.26). And *Brahman* is celebrated as its (world's) source (1.4.27) — and because of the statement of volition (*abhidhyā*). It is the material cause as it is from the *Brahman* that the *jagat* comes into being and in which it is reabsorbed (*Chāndogya Upaniṣad*, 1.9.1). The effects cannot

be absorbed by anything else than their material cause.

I may add a few explanatory remarks:

1.4.26: *The Brahman* is the material cause owing to its transformation. As *Taittirīya Upaniṣad* (2.7) states: "The *ātman* transforms itself into its own Self: That is "The Self got itself transformed into the things of the world." Here it asserts *avikṛta-parināma-vāda*. Transformation with no change in its being). Śaṅkara takes his usual *adhyāsa* view and Bhāskara criticizes Śaṅkara's view as Mahāyānika.

1.4.27: The *Brahman* is 'sung', that is, celebrated as the source of all.

As *BrSū*, 1.4.28 states: 'Hereby all the doctrines opposed to the Vedānta view are explained.[8] A few more points from Vallabha's commentary on these *sūtras* will clarify his point of view:

1.4.23: Vallabhācārya quotes the *Chāndogya Upaniṣad* (6.1.4) and says: 'As the knowledge of a lump of clay — the material cause — leads to the knowledge of all things of clay, the *Brahman* being the material cause of all existing things, its knowledge leads to the knowledge of all.[9]

Conclusion

The world is a reality in the form of the *Brahman*. The *samavāyī kāraṇa* (material cause) is the *Brahman* and not *prakṛti*. (AB Vol. II, p. 975)

1.4.24: As *Taittirīya Upaniṣad*, 2.6.1. states that the *Brahman* had the volition (*abhidhyā*) to be many and it became so. This confirms the truth that the *Brahman* is the material cause of the world. The statement in the *Chāndogya Upaniṣad* (1.9.1) about the origin (*āvirbhāva*), sustenance and annihilation (*tirobhāva*) of the universe from and into the *Brahman* proves *Brahman*'s being the material cause. Vallabhācārya concludes his commentary on that *sūtra* by quoting '*ekatvena pṛthaktvena*', etc., from *BG*, IX.15.

1.4.25: Confirms Brahmā's being the *samavāyī kāraṇa* by quoting *Chāndogya Upaniṣad* (1.9.1) and *BG*, X.8.

1.4.26: *Brahman*'s manifestation is only a change of phase not a *vikāra* (Transformation). The *Brahman*'s transformation into *jagat* is *avikr̥ta-pariṇāma* with no change within it) (Br.) *Brahman*'s transformation of itself shows that it is both the Agent and the effect (*svasya eva karma-kartr̥-bhāvāt*). Vallabhācārya concludes that the world (*kārya* or effect) is a change or transformation of the cause (*Brahman*) and *Brahman* is the material cause of the world.[10]

The Creation or Manifestation and disappearance (destruction) are known as the *āvirbhāva* (manifestation) and *tirobhāva* (obscuration) power of the Brahman. It is like the unfolding (*prasārita*) and folding (*saṁveṣṭita* or *saṁveṣṭana*) of a piece of cloth.

Vallabhācārya has convincingly proved that the *jagat* is the *ādhibhautika* aspect of the *Brahman*. It is identical with the *Brahman* with the aspects of consciousness and Bliss being obscured for the time being.

To Sum Up

The *jagat* is the *ādhibhautik* aspect of the *Brahman*. Through His volition, the *Brahman* became many and manifested Himself as the World. But thereby there is no change (*vikāra*) in Him. This is called *Avikr̥ta-pariṇāma-vāda*. *Jagat* is cognisable and not merely ideational as *vijñāna-vāda* holds. The *Brahman* (a reality) is the cause and the world is the effect but there is no difference between the cause and the effect (*abhinna-nimittopādāna-kāraṇa*). *Jagat* or *prapānca* and *saṁsāra* are different as *saṁsāra* is transient. The so-called 'creation' is the manifestation (*āvirbhāva*) and the 'destruction' is simply (*tirobhāva*). The *jagat* is identical with the *Brahman* with the consciousness aspect and Bliss-aspect temporarily obscured.

Notes

1. आत्मा वा इदमेक अग्र आसीत्, नान्यत् किञ्चन मिषत्, स ईक्षत लोकान्नु सृजा इति।

   — ऐतरेय उपनिषद, 1.1.1

2. सर्वं खल्विदं ब्रह्म।

   — छांदोग्य उपनिषद, 3.14.1

3. विस्फुलिंगा इवाग्नेस्तु सदंशेन जडा अपि।

आनन्दांश-स्वरूपेण सर्वान्तर्यामिरूपिणः।।

— *तदीनि,* I. 28

4. On नाभाव उपलब्धेः (*BrSū*, 2.2.28) Vallabhācārya concludes यस्तु उपलभमान एव नाहमुपलभ इति वदति स कथमुपादेयवचनः स्यात्।

5. नैवं जागरितोपलब्धं वस्तु स्तम्भादिकं कस्याम् अपि अवस्थायां बाध्यते।

— Śaṅkara on *BrSū*, 2.2.29

6. अर्थव्यतिरेकेण वासनाया अभावात् वासनाव्यतिरेकेणापि अर्थोपलब्धेः, अन्वयव्यतिरेकाभ्यामर्थसिद्धिः।

— AB on *BrSū*, 2.2.30

7. नमो भगवते तस्मै कृष्णाय अद्भुतकर्मणे।
रूपनामविभेदेन जगत् क्रीडति यो यतः।।

— *तदीनि,* I.1

8. The text of the *sūtras* mentioned here:
1.4.23: प्रकृतिश्च प्रतिज्ञादृष्टान्तानुपरोधात्।
1.4.24: अभिध्योपदेशाच्च।
1.4.25: साक्षाच्चोभयाम्नात्।
1.4.26: आत्मकृतेः परिणामात्।
1.2.27: योनिश्च हियते।
1.4.28: एतेन सर्वे व्याख्याता व्याख्याताः।

9. भगवान् ज्ञातः . . . सर्वं ज्ञातं भवति। . . . अतो ब्रह्मरूपेण सत्यस्य जगतः ब्रह्मैव समवायिकारणम्।

— AB on *BrSū*, 1.4.29 (Vol. II, pp. 971)

10. तस्माद् ब्रह्मपरिणामलक्षणं कार्यं इति जगत्समवाय-कारणत्वं ब्रह्मण एव सिद्धम्।

—AB on *BrSū*, 1.4.26 (Vol. II, pp. 981)

9

Epilogue

THUS far we have seen how the early man in India was fascinated and mystified by the grandeur of Nature around him. It became a challenge to his intelligence and curiosity. He tried to probe deeply the Reality underlying this miraculous phenomenon.

He reasoned: As nothing comes out of nothing (*asat*), there must be some positive Reality (*sat*) which creates and controls the world. The Upaniṣadic period records such speculations about the nature of the Reality and its relations with Man and the World. In course of time, stray speculations developed into thought-currents which came to be known as Dvaita, Advaita, Viśiṣṭādvaita, etc.

We do not know since when the Reality came to be designated as Śiva of Viṣṇu. But whatever be the name of the Reality and whatever the thought-patterns regarding the relations of the Reality with Man and the World, they had an implicit faith in the validity of the Śruti texts. The *Bhagavad Gītā* though a part of the epic *Mahābhārata*, was unanimously accepted by them as an authoritative text (*prasthāna*) as it contained the essence of Upaniṣads. The third *prasthāna* (Valid authority) accepted by all is the *Śārīraka* or *Brahma Sūtra*, though it is a commentary and a synthesis of the doctrines in Upaniṣads.

The dialogue continued in the post-Upaniṣadic period as can be seen from the records of opinions of the eight *ācāryas* in the pre-*Brahma Sūtra*, yet post-Upaniṣadic period.

In the post-*Brahma Sūtra* period, the dialogue continued vigorously. The land-marks of the debate, the progress in the development of philosphical thought, are associated with the names of the exponents of those doctrines such as *ajāta-vāda* of Gauḍapāda, Advaita (*kevalādvaita*) of Śaṅkara, *bhedābheda-vāda* of Bhāskara, the Viśiṣṭādvaita theory of (Vaiṣṇava) Rāmānuja, the Śaiva Viśiṣṭāvaita (with a tilt to Advaita) of Śrīkaṇṭha, Dvaita of Madhva, the Svābhāvika Bhedābheda of the Vaiṣṇava Nimbārka, the Dvaitādvaita (also called Śakti Viśiṣṭādvaita) of Śrīpati Paṇḍit. These different shades of doctrines form the background of Vallabhācārya's philosophy.

Being a staunch devotee of Kṛṣṇa, Vallabhācārya regards the *Bhāgavata Purāṇa* as the remover of all doubts (*sarva-sandeha-vāraka*). Though he does not call the *Bhāgavata* as the fourth *prasthāna*, he regarded all these four (three *prasthāna*s and the *Bhāgavata Purāṇa*) as constituting a single body of *pramāṇa*s.

The Supreme Reality is Kṛṣṇa or *Brahman*. He is one without a second. By his sheer Will-Power, He creates, sustains, and annihilates the world — in fact He can do anything He wills, without the help of *māyā* or *avidyā*. His Will-Power is not different from Him. This doctrine is known as Śuddhādvaita as it is not 'soiled' by *māyā*. He is the material and instrumental cause of the world, still He is *sat-cit-ānanda* Himself. He is the repository of contradictory qualities like *saguṇa*, *nirguṇa*, etc. It is through His Grace that one can get *mokṣa*. As against Śaṅkara, he firmly declares that as the *Brahman* is real, His creation, the world, is real.

Vallabha is also a proponent of a special kind of *bhakti* called *puṣṭi bhakti*. (See Appendix I)

The *Brahma-Vāda* (Discussion about the *Brahman*) enunciated by Vallabha emphasizes the one-ness of *jaḍa*, *jīva* and *antaryāmin*. Like Rāmānuja he does not condemn the *jaḍa* to eternity. He says that in *jaḍa* (material objects, non-sentient ones) there is the quality of *sat*, i.e existence. In *jīva*, i.e the animated ones, there are two qualities — *sat* (Existence) and *cit* (Consciousness) and in *antaryāmin* (three qualities, viz., *sat*, *cit* and *ānanda*). If the quality *cit* is devdeloped in the *jaḍa*, it becomes animate and with the infusion of *ānanda*, it becomes *antaryāmin*. Vallabha is more liberal than Rāmānuja.

By creating the world out of himself, He (the Lord) transforms himself as *jīva* and *jagat*, like gold transformed into an ornament. This *līlā* (sport) on His part involves no change and hence it is called *avikṛta-pariṇāma-vāda*. The relations between the Lord and the world are both non-different (*ananya*) as effect (created world) is included in the *kāraṇa* (Cause). This is called *satkārya-vāda*. Impartiality of the Lord and the doctrine of Grace or getting *mokṣa* are common to other sects. He regards Kṛṣṇa Himself is *bhagavān*, but for removing internal agonies of people, he incarnates as Datta, Kapila, etc. For removing external calamities, he takes *avatāras* like Divine Fish, Man-lion, etc. When He inspires persons for a particular purpose, that is known as *āvirbhāva*. And as pointed out by him in *TDN*, III. 1.49 the *āvirbhāvas* are equivalent to regular *avatāras*.

We must give credit to Vallabhācārya inviting our attention to the concept of *akṣara Brahman*. According to Vallabhācārya, *akṣara Brahman* is distinct from the *para Brahman* and individual souls emanate from Him like sparks from fire. It is due to the Will of the Lord that, with diminished Bliss (*gaṇitānanda*), the *akṣara Brahman* seems to assume the following four forms:

(1) *Prakṛti* and *Puruṣa*, the cause of everything.

(2) *Kāla* (Time) — It is all-pervasive and the cause of disturbing the equilibruim of *guṇas* of *prakṛti*.

(3) *Karma* — Action, Universal, manifesting itself in different actions.

(4) *Svabhāva* — Producer of change (*pariṇāma-hetutva*). *Akṣara Brahman* contains within himself millions of worlds. As a spiritual form of the *para Brahman*, *akṣara Brahman* incarnates as *puruṣa*. It is by the *upāsanā* (Adoration or *bhakti*) of *akṣara Brahman* that *jñānins* (the knowers of spirituality) become one with the supreme *ātman*.

Vallabhācārya holds that individual souls are atomic, eternal, uncreated, *Brahman* — like, but with Bliss slightly diminished. They are both the Agents and Enjoyers of the fruits of their *karmans*. Hence, God is neither cruel nor partial, when He dispenses the fruits. Vallabhācārya rejects the theory of *adṛṣṭa*.

According to Vallabhācārya the *jagat* is the *ādhibhautika* aspect of the *Brahman*. It is the manifestation of the *Brahman* causing no *vikāra* (Change) in Him (*avikṛta-pariṇāma vāda*). The *Brahman* (A Reality) is the cause of the world. And so there is no difference between Cause and the Effect (*abhinna-nimittopādāna-kāraṇa*), the world is real. The *jagat* (different from the ephemeral *prapañca*) is identical with the *Brahman* with conscious-ness and bliss-aspect temporarily obscured.

To be fair to others, we must acknowledge the fact that some of the dectrines of Vallabhācārya were prevalent before Vallabhācārya. Thus *Brahman*'s possession of attributes, the world as transformation of the *Brahman*, synthesis of *jñāna* and *karma* (*jñāna-karma-samuccaya*), the concept of *bhakti*, the necessity of Divine Grace for Liberation, the need for complete surrender to God (*prapatti*), to mention a few, were already current before Vallabhācārya.

Dr. G.H. Bhatta summarises the exact contribution of Vallabhācārya as follows:

> The doctrine of non-dualism, the conception of God as full of deliciousness (*rasa*) and joy, coexistence of contradictory attributes in *Brahman*, the idea of AKṢARA BRAHMAN, the theory of the creation of the world from the very form (*sva-rūpa*) of *Brahman*, the transformation of the *Brahman* into the world without suffering any change, self-dedication to the Lord, emphasis on God's Grace and the aesthetic and emotional form of devotion, are the special features of Vallabha's teaching.
>
> — *History of Philosophy Eastern and Western*, Vol. I, p. 356

Is the teaching of Vallabhācārya relevant to the modern world? Yes, positively yes. His strong refutation of the demoralising concept of the illusory nature of the world inspired his followers for zest in life. His teaching elevated the life of all sections of the society — a democratic outlook embracing all castes and communities. As G.H. Bhatta notes: "Painting, Music, Sanskrit, Hindi and Gujarati literature flourished under the inspiration of Vallabha's teaching." His message of *bhakti-karma-samuccaya* (Synthesis of *bhakti* and Action) will certainly give solace and guidance to moderns distraught with nerve-racking tensions and frustrations.

Appendix I

Puṣṭi Bhakti

It was a glorious period for the *bhakti Movement*. In addition to Vallabha, we find Madhusūdana Sarasvatī and Gaurāṅga Prabhu Caitanya propagating the *bhakti* Cult in their own light. Vallabhācārya the exponent of Śuddhādvaita, wrote his famous tracts such as *Puṣṭi-pravāha-maryādā-bheda*, *Śrī-Kṛṣṇāśraya*, *Siddhānta-rahasya* and the like. Madhusūdana Sarasvatī, the staunch advocate of Kevalādvaita, the author of the famous work *Advaita-siddhi* wrote the *Bhakti-rasāyana*. Curiously enough Vallabha and Madhusūdana Sarasvatī, the advocate of rival schools of philosophy, were both devotees of Śrī Krsna and personal friends. Gaurāṅga Prabhu Caitanya, the exponent of *Acintya-bhedābheda* did not write any treatise but his desciples like Śrī Rūpa Goswāmī, Sanātana Goswāmī and their disciples of Gauḍīya Vaiṣṇava School richly contributed to *bhakti* literature by works like *Bhakti-rasāmrta-sindhu*, *Hari-bhakti Vilāsa* to mention a few.

In *Puṣṭi-pravāha-maryādā-bheda*, Vallabhācārya classified souls in three categories:[1] (1) *Pravāha*, (2) *Maryādā*, (3) *Puṣṭi*.[2]

(1) *Pravāha* souls are ordinary persons who are involved in the cycle of births and deaths.

(2) *Maryādā* souls observe the Vedic paths with all the prescriptions of duties.

(3) *Puṣṭi bhakta*s are the favoured few who are elected by the Lord in order to shower His grace on them, for which no humanly ostensible reason can be seen. The *puṣṭi bhakta*s may observe prescribed religious duties, but it is not binding on them.[3] This

doctrine of Election is a special feature of Vallabha's system. Devotees of *puṣṭi* type have got natural love for God. They do everything for Lord Kṛṣṇa. The special feature of *puṣṭi bhakti* is that, Love for the Lord is the starting point, while in *maryādā bhakti*, Love for the Lord has to be generated by means of *bhakti* of ninefold path (e.g., meditation, worship, etc.). The *puṣṭi bhakta* is already beyond such attempts as they have Love for God from the beginning. A *puṣṭi bhakta* realises his helplessness and throws himself completely at the feet of the Lord dedicating not only himself but all his belongings, and ignores the duties prescribed by Dharma-Śāstra for his Class (*varṇa*) and Stage in life (*āśrama*).

As *puṣṭi bhakti* of the standard of *Gopīs* of Vṛndāvana is not possible nowadays (even in Vallabha's Period), Vallabhācārya proposes the doctrine of *prapatti* (complete surrender to the will of the Lord):[4] All persons irrespective of class or nationality can reach the goal by sustaining throughout the whole life, the spirit of self-surrender and resignation to the Will of the Lord. Vallabhācārya, is however, opposed to the manner of renunciation of Monistic *saṁnyāsa*. In the *bhakti mārga* renunciation proceeds out of the necessity for proper maintenance of the *bhakti mārga* and NOT as a matter of duty.

The fourth type of *bhakti is śuddha bhakti*. These *bhakta*s have boundless love for God, like *gopīs* of Vṛndāvana and they are rare.

The concept of *puṣṭi bhakti* is a special contribution of Vallabha and is fascinating to all.

Notes

1. पुष्टि-प्रवाह-मर्यादा विशेषेण पृथक् पृथक्।
   जीव-देह-क्रिया-भेदैः प्रवाहेण फलेन च।।

   — *पुष्टि-प्रवाह-मर्यादा-भेद,* 1

2. पोषणं तदनुग्रहः।

   — *भागवतपुराण,* 3.10.4

   अनुग्रहरूपोभगवद्धर्भः पुष्टिः।

   — *प्रमेय रत्नार्णव*

3. यदा यस्यानुगृह्णाति भगवानात्मभावितः।
स जहाति मतिं लोके वेदे च परिनिष्ठिताम्।।

— भागवत, 4.2.6

भगवत्तारतम्येन तारतम्यं भजन्ति हि।
लौकिकत्वं वैदिकत्वं कापटयात् तेषु नान्यथा।।

(apparently)

— *पुष्टि प्रवाह मार्गभेद*, 20

4. ऐहिके पारलोके च सर्वथा शरणं हरिः।
दुःखहानौ तथा पापे भये कामाद्य-पूरणे।।

— *विवेकधैर्याश्रय निरूपण*, 10

Appendix II

Verses attributed to Viṣṇusvāmin

Vallabhācārya expresses his allegiance to Viṣṇusvāmī of Kāñcī, though he was not a direct disciple of the founder of his school. Biographical information about Viṣṇusvāmī is given in *supra* p. 56. The following is a free translation of the verses attributed to Viṣṇusvāmī. It will enable readers to take a comparative view of the philosophy of Viṣṇusvāmī and that of Vallabhācārya.

(1) Veses quoted by Śrīdhara in his Commentary. on the Bhāgavata 1.7.5 & 6[1]

1. The Lord is veritable *sat* (Existence), *cit* (Consciousness) and *ānanda* (Bliss) *incarnate*. He is embraced by his *saṁvit* power called *hlādinī* (Delightgiver), while *jīva* (Individual soul) enmeshed in his nescience (*avidyā*) is a mine of miseries.

2-3. The Lord has *māyā* under his control, while the *jīva* is one who is harassed by her. In Him (Kṛṣṇa) the Supreme Bliss is manifest, while the *jīva* is the experiencer of miseries since his inception (manifestation as *jīva*). Due to *avidyā* the *jīva* has his intelligence spoiled since times immemorial. Being deluded by *māyā*, he entertains difference-proneness and thereby he is affected with fear and misery. We praise Lord Nṛhari (Man-Lion)

The following four more verses are attributed to Viṣṇusvāmin[2]:

1. Comparing the *jīvātman* (individual soul) and the *Brahman* men are exhorted to resort to the Lord.

The *jīvāman* (the individual soul) is *aṇu* (atom). It is separate in every individual and has a very meagre knowledge (*alpajña*). He is the servant of the feet of Hari. Lord Kṛṣṇa is free from all blemishes and is as if a 'flood' of all excellent qualities. He is constituted of consciousness and Bliss. He is the father of god *Brahmā*. O men, take resort unto Him who is full of mercy.

2. Viṣṇusvāmī describes the greatness of Lord and advises men to resort to Him. The verse is a description of the Lord:

   The Lord is a limitless, unfathomable ocean of mercy. He transports *jīvas* across the ocean of *saṁsāra*. He is a support unto people who bow to Him with their heads. He is always accessible through devotion. He is ever-ready to confer grace on persons who are lovingly devoted to Him. The Son of Nanda (Lord Kṛṣṇa), who is served by gods, is constituted of consciousness and Bliss. Take resort unto Him.

3. This verse expresses the strong desire of Viṣṇusvāmī to visualize the Lord: There is no philosophical point for discussion but a craving to see the Lord:

   When can I see Kṛṣṇa in the lap of Yośodā or frisking in the presence of Nanda, the Chief of Vraja.

   When can I see Him playing delightfully with all his friends (including his brother Balarāma) on the bank of the Yamunā (lit. the daughter of the Sun-god).

4. Viṣṇusvāmī expresses regrets towards the aversion of men to the Lord by whose grace the curtain of *māyā* is removed and God becomes manifest:

   People of *asura* (demon-like) mentality do not know you (O Lord) though you are so well-known in all Śāstras. Your *māyā* makes them (revolve) wander excessively through the cycle of births and death.

But those who are yours, (your devotees) are full of love for you, can visualize you directly with ease, as the curtain of *māyā* is automatically removed.

The Following Traditional Verse is said to sum up Viṣṇusvāmī's Teaching[3]:

1. In the opinion (school) of Viṣṇusvāmī, Kṛṣṇa is *Brahman* itself constituting *sat* (existence) and *cit* (consciousness). He manifests Himself in Gokula out of Pure Free Will.

Service unto Kṛṣṇa (the enemy of demon Madhu) is said to be *mukti* (Liberation). His grace helps to attain it (*mukti*). Followers of Hari become free from (devoid of) *avidyā*. The world is real and one with the *Brahman*.

(The last sentence is noted as "*avikṛta-pariṇāma-vāda* of Śuddhādvaitism".)

Notes

1. *Verses quoted by Śrīdhara in his Commentary. on the Bhāgavata Purāna,* I.7.5I6

(1) ह्लादिन्या संविदाश्लिष्टः सच्चिदानन्द ईश्वरः।
स्वाविद्यासंवृतो जीवः संक्लेशनिकराकरः।।

(2) स ईशो यद्वशे माया स जीवो यस्तयार्दितः।
स्वाविर्भूतपरानन्दः स्वाविर्भूतसुदःख भूः।।

(3) स्वादृगुत्य विपर्यास-भवभेदजभीशुचः ।
यन्मायया जुषन्नास्ते तमिमं नृहरिं नुभः।।

2. *Four move verses Traditionally attributed to Viṣṇusvāmī*

(1) अणुं जीवात्मानं हरिचरणदासं न जननम्।
विभिन्नं जानीत प्रतितनु संज्ञानाशविभवम्।।
चिदानन्दाकारं व्रजपतिकुमारं क-जनकम्।
गुणौघं निर्दोषं भजत मनुजा ब्रह्म सदयम्।।

(2) कृपापारावारं भवजलधिपारं सुखकरम्।
जनानामाधारं प्रणतशिरसा शान्त-मनसाम्।।
सदा भक्त्या लभ्यं प्रणयपरयानुग्रहपरम् ।
चिदानन्दं नन्दात्मजममरसेव्यं श्रयतभोः।

(3) कदा बालं कृष्णं सखिभिरखिलैः साग्रजमहम्।
मिलित्वा खेलन्तं तरणितनयोरोधसि मुदा।।
यशोदायाः क्रोडे व्रजपतिपुरः क्वापि ललितम्।
विराजं राजन्तं नयनपथमाप्तास्मि समुदम्।।

(4) न जानन्त्येव त्वामसुरमतयः शास्त्रविदितम्।
त्वदीया माया तान् भ्रमयति नितान्तं व्रजपते।।
त्वदीयास्त्वामेव प्रणयभरशैथिल्यमनसो।
निरीक्षन्ते साक्षात् त्वदपगतमायाजवनिका।।

3. *A traditional Verse summarising Viṣṇusvāmin's Teaching*

विष्णुस्वामि-मते व्रजेशतनयः श्रीब्रह्मसच्चिन्मयः।
शुद्धेच्छावशतो जनाननुगतः प्रादुर्भवत् गोकुले।।
मुक्तिर्दास्यमितीरितं मधुरिपोस्तत्साधकोऽनुग्रहः।
स्वाविद्यारहिता हरेरनुचरा ब्रह्मात्मकं सज्जगत्।।

Source: *श्रीमद्वल्लभाचार्य-व्यक्तकित्व सिद्धान्त और सन्देश* डॉ. गजाननशर्मा विरचित, pp. 41-47
वैष्णव मित्रमंडल, इंदौर द्वारा प्रकाशित, 1981.

Bibliography

Abhinavagupta, *Tantra-sāra*, Kashmir Sanskrit Series (KSS), Srinagar, 1918,

———, *Tantrāloka* (with Jayaratha's commentary), KSS.

Ali, S.M., *The Geography of the Purāṇas*, Bombay, Peoples Publishing House, 1973.

Bhāgavad Gītā, (with 18 commentaries) Gujarathi Printing Press, Bombay.

Bhāgavata Purāṇa (with 15 commentaries) Bhāgavata Vīdyapīṭha, Ahmedabad.

Dasgupta, S.N., *History of Indian Philosophy*, Vol. IV, Delhi, Motilal Banarsidass.

Dhruva, B.M., *An Introduction to the Śuddhādvaita School of Philosophy of Śrī Vallabhācārya* (self-published) 1950.

Gauḍapāda, *Māṇḍūkya Kārikā*.

Giridhara, *Śuddhādvaita Mārtaṇḍa*.

Hastings, *Encyclopaedia of Religion and Ethics*.

History and Culture of Indian People, Vol. Delhi Sultanate, Bombay, Bharatiya Vidya Bhavan.

Karamarkar, R.D., *Rāmānuja's Śrī Bhāṣya* (with English translation), Pune, University of Pune, 1964.

Madhvācārya, Com. on the *Brahma Sūtra* (with *Tattva-prakāśikā*) with Marāṭhī translation by Rangacarya Raddi, Pune, 1949.

Pagdi, Sethumadhavrao, *Sūfi Sampradāya* (Marāṭhī).

Pande, K.C., *Abhinavagupta: An Historical and Philosophical Study*, Chowkhambha Sanskrit Series, Banaras, 1963.

———, *Bhāskarī*, Vols. I-III, Lucknow University.

Patañjali, *Vyākaraṇa Mahābhāṣya*, Keilhorn.

Phatak, N.R., *Eknāth: Vāṅgmaya and Kārya* (Marāṭhī).

Purāṇas, Gurumaṇḍala editions, Calcutta.

Radhakrishnan, S., *Brahma Sūtra* (Translation exposition, etc.) London, George Allen & Unwin, 1960.

———, (ed.), *History of Pilosophy, Eastern and Western*, Vol. I, London, George Allen & Unwin, 1967.

Śaṅkarācārya, *Śārīraka Bhāṣya on the Brahma Sūtras*, Bombay, Nirnaya Sagar Press, 1904.

Sharma, Gajanan, *Srīmad Vallabhācārya-Vyaktitva aur Sandesh* (Hindī), 1981.

Smṛtis, Gurumaṇḍala editions, Calcutta.

Śrīkaṇṭha, *Brahma Mīmāṁsā Bhāṣya*, Ed. Halasyanath Shastri, Kumbhakonam, Vol. I, 1908, Vol. II, 1918.

Srinivasachari, P.N., *Philosophy of Bhedābheda*, Madras, 1950.

Śrīpati Paṇḍit, *Śrīkara Bhāṣya on the Brahma Sūtras*, ed. by Hayavadanrao, Bangalore, 1937.

Surya Narayana Shastri, *Śivādvaita of Śrīkaṇṭha*, Madras, Madras University, 1930, 1952.

Tagare, G.V., *Śaiva-darshan* (Marāṭhī), Pune, Continental, 1987.

———, *Śiva-Sūtra of Vasugupta* (Marāṭhī) Impressions, Belgaum, 1996.

Upaniṣat-saṅgraha, J.L., Shastri, Delhi, Motilal Banarasidass, 1970.

Vallabhācārya, All works of Vallabhācārya (used here) are published by Vallabha Vidyapeeth, Kolhapur.

———, *Aṇubhāṣya on the Brahma Sūtras* ,Vols. I-V.

———, *Patrāvalaṁbana*, V.S. 2052.

———, *Ṣoḍaśa Granthas*, Vols. I-II.

———, *Tattvārtha-dīpa-nibandha*, Vols. I-III.

Vedas, Text as published by Svādhyāya Maṇḍal, Aundh.

Glossary of Sanskrit Terms

Ābhinna-nimittopādāna-kāraṇa — The doctrine that *Brahman*, the cause of the world is non-differentiated Instrumental-material cause. As the cause, the *Brahman* is real, the world is real.

Abhivyakti — manifestation

Ādhibhautika — pertaining to *bhūtas* (gross elements). For example, Vallabha regards the world as the *ādhibhautika* form of the *Brahman*. This is the third grade or aspect of the *Brahman*.

Ādhidaivika — The first grade of the *Brahman*.

The *Para Brahman par excellence* or Kṛṣṇa or Puruṣottama according to Vallabha.

Adhikaraṇa — A section of a *Sūtra* work. It consists of five factors: *Viṣaya* (subject-matter), *Viṣaya* (doubt) *Pūrva-pakṣa* (statement of objection), *Siddhānta* (established decision), *Saṅgati* (connection with other sections).

Ādhyātmika — second grade of *Brahman*: The *akṣara Brahman*.

Adṛṣṭa — The effect of the past *karmas* unseen in the present birth. This is the theory proposed by Mīmāṁsakas.

Advaita — non-difference, identity between the *Brahman*, individual soul and the world. (Śaṅkara's theory: *Kevalādavita*).

Advayavāda — The full term '*īśvarādvayavāda*' — Parama-śiva is non-different from individual souls and the world. The term is used in Kāśmīr Śaivism.

Antaryāmin — the Principle dwelling in finite souls.

Apūrva — the (prospective) fruit of a religious act.

Asparśa Yoga — Gauḍapāda's term for Advaita Vedānta.

Asura-vyāmoha līlā — A term in *Puṣṭi mārga* for Vallabhācārya's *Samādhi.*

A-vikṛta-pariṇāmavāda — The doctrine that no change (*vikāra*) occurs when the *Brahman* becomes many and manifested Himself as the world.

Āvirbhāva — manifestation (creation) of the world as against *tirobhāva* (or *pralaya*) which is obscuration of the world. The world is not destroyed. It is manifested and concealed or withdrawn within God.

Bheda — difference. *Bheda-pratyakṣa* — difference between God and the soul is a matter of experience according to Vaiṣṇava and Śaiva (Siddhānta Śaiva) dualists.

Bhedābheda — The doctrine of difference-cum-non-difference between God and the world. This doctrine was promulgated by Auḍulomi and later endorsed by Bhāskara.

Brahma-samavāyīkāraṇa — *Brahman* as the *samavāyī* cause of the world.

Cit — consciousness. The characteristic of the animate world. *Sat-cit-ānanda* are the constituents of the *Brahman.* Kāśmīrī Śaivas use the term *cidānanda*, for they say that without *sat* (existence), the next two *cit* and *ānanda* are impossible.

Dharma — a quality.

Dharma — a religion.

Dharma-sabhā — A conference of *paṇḍits* (Sanskrit scholars) to discuss some religious topic.

Dharma-śāstra — codes of behaviour, law, Smṛti works.

Dharma-śāstra-kāra — author of works on Dharma Śāstra, originally applied to the authors of Smṛti works. Later extended to qualified scholars who gave decisions on social and religious problems.

Dharmin — possessor of quality.

Dvaita — The doctrine that regards God or *Brahman*, individual souls and the world are different *inter se.* This was held both by followers of Madhva and Śaiva Siddhāntins.

Jaḍa — non-sentients, matter.

Jīva, Jīvātman — the individual soul.

Kāraṇa — cause, source.

Laya — merger. *BrSū*, 4.2.1 states that *vāk* (power of speech) merges in the mind. Rāmānuja interprets here *laya* as 'association' while Śaṅkara says it is *vṛtti-laya* 'merging' as the power of speech and not *svarūpa-laya* — a view endorsed by Śrīkaṇṭha.

Mahāvākya — The great statement, the essence of the Veda, e.g. *tat tvam asi* which is interpreted as "Thou are that" i.e. *Brahman*.

Mauñjī bandhana or *Upanayana* — A ceremony to initiate a boy in Vedic studies. It is called *mauñjī bandhana* as a girdle of *muñja* grass is bound round the waist of the boy for loincloth. The sacred thead of *yajñopavīta* is worn on the boy's person and the *gāyatrī mantra* is imparted to him at this time. This ceremony is regarded as a second birth (the first being the natural birth). Boys belonging to the brāhmaṇa, kṣatriya and vaiśya communities were eligible for this ceremony. After thc performance of the ceremony, the boys were called *dvijas* (twice-born ones).

The ceremony is called *Upanayana* as the boy is 'brought near to' i.e. entrusted to the teacher for education.

Mantra — sacred formula of letters of esoteric nature. For example *oṁ namaḥ śivāya* for Śaivas, *śrīkṛṣṇaḥ śaraṇam mana* for followers of Vallabha; some Śākta *mantras* begin with unintelligible syllables *oṁ hrāṁ hrīṁ* etc.

Māyā — Illusion. Illusive power of God. *Māyā* is supposed to delude men away from the path of God-realisation. In Śaṅkara's writing *māyā* denotes the following: (1) The phenomenal character of the world. (2) Incomprehensibility of the relation between the *Brahman* and the world of plurality. (3) The principle assumed to account for the appearance of the Brahmā as the world. Īśvara's power for self-expression. The concept appears to be similar to Nāgārjuna's concept of Reality but it is not the same as Nāgārjuna's.

Nibandha-kāras — Writers on digests on topics in Dharmaśāstra. These digests are mainly based on Smṛti works.

Nimitta-kāraṇa — Instrumental cause.

Pradeśa — a span — Dimension of the *Brahman* accommodated in the span-limited space of the heart.

Prakāśa — Knowledge — Paramśiva is both *prkāśa* and *vimarśa* (power).

Pralaya — Withdrawal of the world within God. The world is thus destroyed at the end of a *kalpa*.

Pramā — True knowledge.

Pramāṇa — Valid means of knowledge — the unfailing source of true knowledge (according to Nyāya-Vaiśeṣikas).

Number of Pramāṇas (according to schools of Philosophy): (1) Cārvākas — *Pratyakṣa* (perception); (2) Vaiśeṣikas : (a) *Pratyakṣa* and (b) *Anumāna* (Inference); (3) Sāṁkhyas : add the 3rd *prmāṇa* (c) *Śabda* (testimony); (4) Naiyāyikas : (i) *Pratyakṣa* (ii) *anumāna* (iii) *Upamāna* (comparison, Analogy), *śabda*; (5) Bhaṭṭa Mīmāṁ-sakas add: *arthāpatti* (initial doubt); (6) Kumārila Bhaṭṭa adds *anupalabdhi* (*non-perception*) as the sixth *pramāṇa*.

These can be reduced to three *pramāṇas*: (1) *pratyakṣa* — to include *pratyakṣa* and *anupalabdhi*; (2) *anumāna* — to include *amumāna*, *upamāna* and *arthāpatti*; (3) *śabda*.

Prameya — The Ultimate Reality ascertained by *pramāṇas*, the *Brahman*, Kṛṣṇa (according to Vallabha).

Prasthāna — 'Foundation' — The basic texts, the foundation of philosophy.

They consis of : (1) Ancient Upaniṣads (some ten in number); (2) The *Bhagavad Gītā*; (3) The *Brahma Sūtra*.

To these Vallabha adds : (4) The *Bhāgavata Purāṇa*, especially its *samādhi bhāṣā*.

Pūrva-mīmāṁsā — Mīmāṁsā Sūtras were once regarded as one text. The first part is called *Pūrvamīmāṁsā*. It deals with the sacrificial ritual. Jaimini is regarded as the author of these *sūtras*. It is also a philosophical work. Jaimini's followers Kumārila Bhaṭṭa and Prabhākara Bhaṭṭa founded their own schools. The special contribution of this school is the formulation of logical rules of exact interpretations. These canons were accepted by modern courts to interpret Law.

Puṣṭi mārga — The special form of *bhakti* introduced by Vallabhācārya. It is the doctrine of election by Kṛṣṇa or God of His *bhaktas*. Such favoured *bhaktas* are called *puṣṭi bhaktas*.

Siddha — 'One who has accomplished the highest spiritual wisdom'. In the post-Mahāyāna period, sects of *siddhas* claiming super-natural powers arose amongst Buddhists, Śaivas and Śāktas. Due to their claim to super-natural powers, they weilded great influence on the masses. With the exception of *yogīs* like Matsyendranāth, Gorakhnāth who have contributed to Yogic literature, most of the so-called *siddhas* were privileged beggars. Hazari Prasad Dwivedi's *Nāth sāmpradāya* and Dharma-vira Bharati's *siddha sādhitya* evaluate the positive contribution of the *siddhas* to Indian culture.

Smṛti — Ancient law-books of Hindus. They are written by a number of sages like Manu, Yājñavalkya *et al.*

Śruti — Vedic literature consisting of Vedas, Brāhmaṇas, Āraṇyakas and Upaniṣads (old strata).

Soul — see subject-index.

Svatantra : Indiependent of any external help — can create or destroy the world at one's Free Will.

Tantra (also called Āgama) — Esoteric works guiding performance of secret rites for attaining *siddhi*. (Some spiritual powers or vision of the deity.) The *Tantras* were written by Buddhist, Śaiva and Śākta writers. The obnoxious prctices of some *Tantra*-followers made them unpopular with decent people. *Tantra* practitioners still have a hold on the masses.

Upādāna kāraṇa — The material cause.

Upanayana — see *Mauñjī bandhana.*

Upaniṣads — Ancient philosophical works of Hindus. They are intimate dicourses between a teacher and a pupil or father and his son. They constitute the last part of Śruti Texts.

Varṇa — One of the four divisions of ancient Hindu society. *Varṇas* are four in number: brāhmaṇa, kṣatriya, vaiśya and śūdra. *Varṇa* is a wider term than 'caste'.

Vijñānavāda — The Buddhist doctrine that denies real existence to the world. It is the ideational existence of objects in our mind that we call the world.

Vivarta-vāda — '*Vivarta*' means 'apparent modification'. The world is only 'apparent modification' of the *Brahman*. The *Brahman* is thus the ultimate reality. *BrSū*, II 3.50 and, III.2 16 support the *vivarta vāda* (the world as an apparent modification of the *Brahman*) and not *pariṇāma vāda* (the actual modification of the *Brahman*).

Viśiṣṭādvaita — The doctrine that recognizes the distinction between *cit* (sentients) and *a-cit* (non-sentients) but regards both as parts of God's person. The theory which regards both sentinents (*cit*) and the non-sentinent (*acit*) as parts of God's person. The theory was popularized by Rāmānuja.

Viśva-maya — Immanent in the Universe.

Viśvottīrṇa — Transcendent to the Universe.

Subject-Index

(figures after a subtopic represent page numbers)

General Index